Plain & Elegant
Rich & Common

# Plain & Elegant
# Rich & Common

## Documented New Hampshire
## Furniture, 1750 – 1850

*A Loan Exhibition*

*29 September through 3 November 1978*

NEW HAMPSHIRE HISTORICAL SOCIETY

CONCORD, NEW HAMPSHIRE

This exhibition and catalogue are supported in part by a grant from the National Endowment for the Arts in Washington, D.C., a federal agency.

ISBN 0–915916–09–6

Library of Congress Cataloging in Publication Data

New Hampshire Historical Society.
Plain & elegant, rich & common.

1. Furniture—New Hampshire—History—18th century—Exhibitions.
2. Furniture, Colonial—New Hampshire—Exhibitions.
3. Furniture—New Hampshire—History—19th century—Exhibitions.
I. Title.
NK2435.N4N48   1979      749.2'142'07414272
ISBN 0–915916–09–6      79–13568

All photography is by Bill Finney, Concord, New Hampshire, except for the following: 5, chair, Robert Swenson; 15, high chest and detail, courtesy of the Henry Francis duPont Winterthur Museum; 19, desk and bookcase, Frank Kelly; 19, label, Charles S. Parsons; 23, chest, courtesy of Sotheby-Parke Bernet, Inc., New York; 23, signature, anonymous owner; 34, label, courtesy of the Metropolitan Museum of Art; 36, card table and detail, Joseph Szaszfai; 36, signature, Charles F. Montgomery.

# Table of Contents

# Technical Procedures

ARRANGEMENT   The furniture in this catalogue has been grouped by region, each region being defined by concentrations of population as shown in census returns. Since centers of population in New Hampshire before 1800 were closely related to major river systems, these regions have been identified by the names of rivers. Stylistic differences between the furniture of the several regions have generally not been found to exist, but the arrangement of furniture by region is intended to indicate the strong correlation between cabinetmaking and relatively dense concentrations of population within the state.

WOOD IDENTIFICATION   Woods have been identified by careful examination with naked eye; microscopic examination has not been used owing to limitations of time and funds.

DIMENSIONS   Dimensions are given for each piece as illustrated, and include finials or other terminals if shown. Pieces with movable leaves or writing surfaces have generally been measured closed. Measurements were taken from the extreme points of each piece, and may be visualized as representing the inside dimensions of a box that would exactly contain the object. When necessary, English measurements have been rounded off to the next one-eighth inch; metric measurements have been rounded off to the next millimeter.

CITATIONS   Sources have not been cited in full in catalogue entries and biographical sketches; this information is on file at the New Hampshire Historical Society.

* An asterisk indicates that the piece was not included in the exhibition.

Catalogue by Donna-Belle Garvin, James L. Garvin, and John F. Page

# Lenders to the Exhibition

Rhoda Shaw Clark

George L. Coombs

Daniel J. and Mary Frank Fox

Dr. Benjamin A. Hewitt

Historical Society of Amherst, New Hampshire, Inc.

Brenda Zinn Joziatis

Mr. and Mrs. Warren E. Legsdin

Bertram K. and Nina Fletcher Little

Mr. and Mrs. John W. F. Lloyd

Manchester Historic Association

Metropolitian Museum of Art

Old Sturbridge Village

Dwight E. Robinson and Lucy Grosvenor Robinson

Society for the Preservation of New England Antiquities

Mr. and Mrs. A. H. Steenburgh

Mr. and Mrs. Robert Taft

And several anonymous lenders

# Acknowledgments

This exhibition is an outgrowth of three exhibits in recent years which have focused in some part on New Hampshire furniture. The first of these, "The Decorative Arts of New Hampshire, 1725–1825," mounted at the Currier Gallery in 1964, included several documented pieces and began the difficult task of defining a New Hampshire style. In 1970 "The Dunlaps and Their Furniture," also at the Currier, explored the distinctive contributions of this talented cabinetmaking family, drawing on the extensive researches of Charles S. Parsons. Three years later "The Decorative Arts of New Hampshire: A Sesquicentennial Exhibition" at the Historical Society included a representative sampling of the Society's holdings of New Hampshire furniture.

In the intervening years significant additions have been made to the Society's collection of documented furniture—both by gift and purchase—and by the discovery of documentation for previously anonymous pieces. Thanks largely to the tireless and omnivorous researches of Charles S. Parsons, an honorary trustee of the Historical Society, many documented pieces in public and private collections have also been tracked down and authenticated. As always, Mr. Parsons has freely made available the information he has collected over a long period of years; without his help and enthusiasm our task would have been much more difficult.

Development of this exhibition began more than two years ago when James Garvin wrote the proposal which was ultimately funded by the National Endowment for the Arts. The "grant period" allowed barely a year to complete the exhibition and catalogue; too late we learned that the time proposed was insufficient to work up an exhibition and catalogue of this magnitude without sacrificing other work and without maintaining an impossible schedule. Our task was eased by the willing cooperation of librarians, curators, collectors and friends too numerous to mention individually, and by the cooperation of the news media in publicizing our interest and our plans.

Without the dedicated efforts of the Society's staff the project could never have been completed. Harriet Lacy, Philip Zea and William Copeley bore heavy responsibility for research, Ruth Page meticulously edited copy for the catalogue, and Rita Camp typed endless drafts. Special thanks go to Frank Mevers for his assistance in locating the long-sought bills for the original furnishings of the New Hampshire State House. The many contributions of these and other members of the staff can only be insufficiently recognized; suffice it to say that whatever assistance was needed in any phase of the preparations was willingly forthcoming.

We were fortunate to have the able and sympathetic assistance of Albert B. Gregory of Boston in designing the exhibition and the accompanying gallery guide. A master of diplomacy as well as design, he quickly and effectively translated the staff's vague hopes for the exhibition into concrete and beautiful form. Preparation of the catalogue has been eased through the understanding and talent of Stephen Harvard of The Stinehour Press, whose initial enthusiasm for the project has not waned with the long delay in producing final copy.

We are, of course, especially grateful to our lenders, including the many who have chosen to remain anonymous. All have been enthusiastic in their support of the exhibition and generous in their willingness to share the treasures in their care with an appreciative public.

Special thanks go to William Nathaniel Banks of the W. N. Banks Foundation, to Winthrop L. Carter of the Elizabeth B. Carter Foundation, to David F. Putnam of the Putnam Foundation, to David Gosselin of Wheelabrator-Frye, Incorporated, and to Miss Anna Stearns for generous support of the exhibition and catalogue. Without their help, and the subsidy provided by the National Endowment for the Arts, there would have been no exhibition.

Even as the show was ready to open, new discoveries were being made which will render some of what is said here obsolete. Nevertheless we hope that this catalogue represents a lasting contribution to the study of New Hampshire furniture.

*John F. Page*
DIRECTOR

# Introduction

Writing in 1791, Jeremy Belknap, New Hampshire's first historian, outlined his specifications for the ideal New Hampshire town. "Were I to form a picture of a happy society," Belknap wrote,

> it would be a town consisting of a due mixture of hills, valleys and streams of water: The land well fenced and cultivated; the roads and bridges in good repair; . . . The inhabitants mostly husbandmen; . . . a suitable proportion of handicraft workmen, and two or three traders. . . . A school master who should understand his business and teach his pupils to govern themselves. A social library, annually increasing, and under good regulation. A club of sensible men, seeking mutual improvement. A decent musical society. . . . Such a situation may be considered as the most favorable to social happiness of any which this world can afford (*History of New-Hampshire*, III, p. 251).

The New Hampshire towns in which cabinetmaking flourished almost invariably met Belknap's specifications for the perfect community. The prosperity of these settlements, and ultimately their ability to produce fine furniture and other handicrafts, derived from their geology and geography—their "due mixture of hills, valleys and streams of water." Valleys and streams were especially important to settlers, whose very survival depended upon their ability to identify and cultivate those rare deposits of earth which would yield abundant crops in a predominantly post-glacial landscape and a harsh climate. New Hampshire was not settled in a uniform tide of migration to all parts of its territory. Rather, as the accompanying maps show, settlers congregated in or near low-lying areas which geologists have identified as the beds of ancient glacial lakes and which, in post-glacial times, have become fertile alluvial valleys. As land in such areas became "well fenced and cultivated," agricultural prosperity spurred rapid population growth, local pride, and the need for "a suitable proportion of handicraft workmen" to produce such visible manifestations of success as fine buildings and furniture.

As the best-favored towns began producing an agricultural surplus, it became increasingly important to reach distant trading centers. In an energetic period of internal improvements beginning about 1795, a network of turnpikes was constructed between the most prosperous towns, further assuring their growth and prominence. By 1805 turnpikes and improved bridges connected Portsmouth, Concord, Boscawen, Salisbury, Gilmanton, Canaan, Lebanon, Hanover, Lyme, Orford, Plymouth, and Haverhill. Other highways extended from Amherst northwest to Newport and Claremont, and from New Ipswich to Jaffrey, Keene, Charlestown, and Walpole. It is no accident that the communities whose good soils had already led to strong patterns of settlement became magnets for the improved roads that guaranteed their future prosperity.

The rivers that had initially attracted settlers to New Hampshire's most productive regions were often potentially important to the growth of commerce. This was especially true in the Merrimack Valley, which had become the state's most populous region by 1800. The Middlesex Canal, completed in 1803, connected the lower Merrimack with Boston and presented the opportunity for a direct link between communities in the Concord area and the chief city of New England. A series of rapids or falls, which had created the fertile intervals of the Merrimack and originally encouraged settlement, hampered the transformation of the river into a central waterway for New Hampshire. The falls were by-passed by canals, beginning with Samuel Blodgett's famous Amoskeag Canal, completed in 1807. The river was opened to traffic between Boston and Concord in 1814. During this same period, the towns of the Merrimack Valley were producing an increasing amount of fine cabinetwork; more examples of documented furniture have been found in the Merrimack Valley than in any other portion of the state.

The inhabitants of New Hampshire's chief towns did not neglect the intellectual life, and their increasing level of education was often reflected in noticeably cosmopolitan taste and in patronage of fine cabinetwork. Social libraries, so highly regarded by Jeremy Belknap, were privately-owned institutions used by their members. The first such library in New Hampshire was established in Portsmouth in 1750, and by 1820 some one hundred eighty had been organized in the state. Among the earliest social libraries were those in Amherst, Concord, Gilmanton, Haverhill, Hopkinton, Keene, New Ipswich, and Salisbury, towns that produced much of the furniture seen in this catalogue. Several of New Hampshire's most prosperous towns also supported the type of musical societies recommended by Belknap. Of even greater importance were private academies, which raised the level of education beyond that afforded by the public schools. By 1815 academies had been established in fourteen towns, including Amherst, Charlestown, Exeter, Gilmanton, Haverhill, Londonderry, New Ipswich, Portsmouth, and Salisbury—all of them major cabinetmaking centers in their respective regions. By 1820 newspapers had been started in Amherst, Concord, Dover, Gilmanton, Hanover, Haverhill, Keene, Portsmouth, and Walpole. Many of these same towns supported book publishers and binders; they were also natural centers for judicial proceedings and county government. Each was also the home of several skilled cabinetmakers.

Belknap's "clubs of sensible men, seeking mutual improvement," took a variety of forms in New Hampshire. Of greatest benefit to trades-

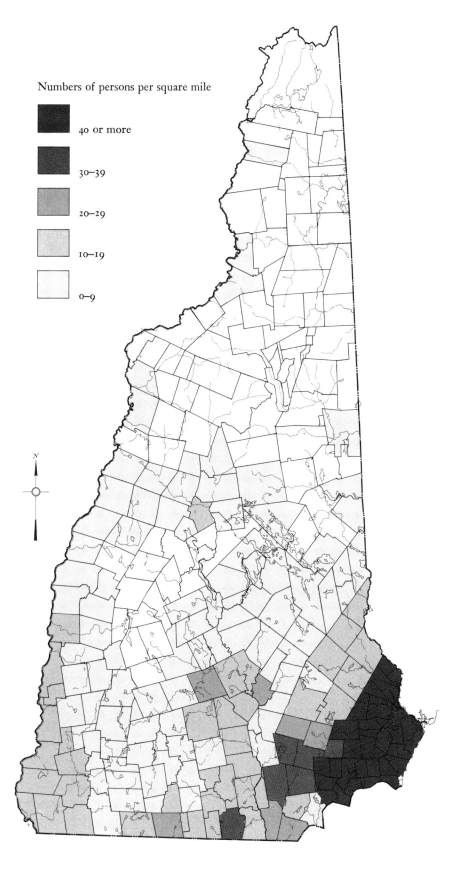

Numbers of persons per square mile

40 or more

30–39

20–29

10–19

0–9

N

Population density in New Hampshire in 1773, based on the census returns of that year. Data
are superimposed on a map compiled by the New Hampshire Department of Resources and
Economic Development from information supplied by the United States Geological Survey.

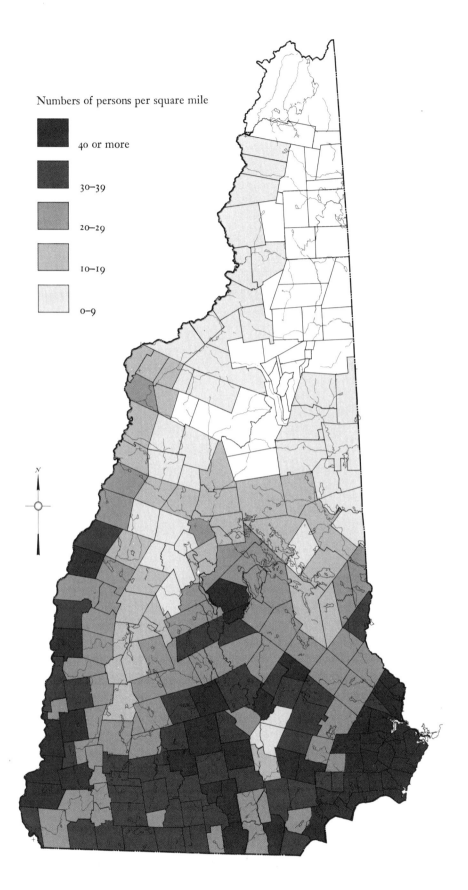

Numbers of persons per square mile

40 or more

30–39

20–29

10–19

0–9

N

Population density in New Hampshire in 1800, based on the census returns of that year. Data are superimposed on a map compiled by the New Hampshire Department of Resources and Economic Development from information supplied by the United States Geological Survey.

men was the Associated Mechanics and Manufacturers of the State of New Hampshire, incorporated in 1803 by men of many trades for "promoting and encouraging industry, good habits, an increase of knowledge in the arts they profess and practice, and their common interest." Among the first members were cabinetmakers Langley Boardman and Ebenezer Clifford, and chairmaker Josiah Folsom.

Intellectual and material culture are both expressions of a society that has passed the state of hardship and can begin to nuture the amenities of life. It is no coincidence, then, that most of the towns that supported such cultural institutions as academies, libraries, printing offices, and self-improvement societies also produced and patronized fine cabinetwork. Those New Hampshire towns in which the greatest number of cabinetmakers are known to have worked before 1825 are Amherst, Bedford, Boscawen, Charlestown, Concord, Dover, Exeter, Haverhill, Hopkinton, Keene, Milford, New Ipswich, Newport, Portsmouth, Salisbury, Sanbornton, Walpole, and Weare—much the same group that achieved prominence and productivity in other respects.

New Hampshire cabinetmaking occurred primarily in geographically coherent regions of the state: the Piscataqua area; the Merrimack Valley; the valleys of the Contoocook and Souhegan Rivers (themselves tributaries of the Merrimack); the Connecticut Valley; and the Saco Valley. The most important features of these regions, in which the influx and growth of New Hampshire's population were concentrated, are major rivers or systems of smaller streams. The fertile soils of the river valleys attracted settlers, assured prosperity, and eventually supported the production of fine architecture and furniture.

Because these regions are defined by geographical rather than political boundaries, the concept of New Hampshire furniture is in many ways an artificial one. New Hampshire is not a single geographical or cultural entity, nor do its principal areas of population belong to it alone. The Piscataqua region lies almost as much in Maine as in New Hampshire, and many of its cultural contacts were with coastal communities elsewhere in New England rather than with inland New Hampshire. The older, lower regions of the Merrimack Valley, from which much of the culture and population of the upper valley were derived, lie in Massachusetts. The same is true of the Connecticut Valley, except that here the origins of the population extend even further south to Connecticut, while the upper river valley and its sophisticated handicrafts belong equally to Vermont and New Hampshire. The Saco Valley lies mostly in Maine, and the greatest flowering of its material culture occurred along the Maine coast.

Moreover, the individuals who marked their furniture have been found in many cases to have come to their respective towns from outside the state, or to have served an apprenticeship in a different town from the one in which they eventually settled. More than thirty percent of the cabinetmakers represented in this catalogue were born and trained outside of New Hampshire, and some left the state after working in it for varying periods. Like their yeoman counterparts, these men were frequently on the move, restlessly seeking a better life. By the time of the Revolution, only a minority of New Hampshire's population could claim descent from the early settlers of the Piscataqua area. The remainder derived from Massachusetts, Connecticut, or foreign stock. It is not surprising that the descendants of these settlers retained contact with their kinsmen in Massachusetts or elsewhere, or that cabinetmakers from outside the state often sought new homes and markets in prosperous New Hampshire communities where friends or relatives had settled. These men acted as carriers of a regional aesthetic rather than as representatives of strong localized cultures.

Thus, although the patterns of New Hampshire's settlement and growth relate closely to the several principal river systems of the state, it cannot be said that a distinctive culture developed in each region. It is true that different groups tended to predominate in each area. Jeremy Belknap noted that the settlers of New Hampshire "might have been divided into three classes. Those of the old towns [of the seacoast], and the migrants from them. Those on the southern border, most of whom were emigrants from Massachusetts; and those on the Connecticut river, who came chiefly from Connecticut" (*History*, III, p. 191). More recent historians have identified another group, the Scots-Irish. These were Scottish Presbyterians from northern Ireland who, migrating from their early settlements around Worcester, Massachusetts, and in Londonderry, New Hampshire, added a substantial element to the population of the lower Merrimack, Contoocook, and Connecticut river valleys.

In each region the mixture of people of various origins was assured by the policy of both New Hampshire and Massachusetts of granting townships to almost any group that petitioned for land. Furthermore, except for a few towns adjacent to the seacoast and in the southern river valleys, New Hampshire was settled late—only forty to sixty years before the date of most of the furniture in this catalogue. The rapid improvement in trade and communication by this period quickly overcame isolation, which is necessary for the development of distinctive regional cultures. As a result, most New Hampshire furniture reflects a common aesthetic that seems to have pervaded the well-settled areas of New England by the late eighteenth century.

The furniture in this catalogue does not lend itself, then, to classification by cultural traits. Documented furniture by its very nature proclaims itself the product of self-conscious artisans; as the work of individual cabinetmakers, it is best studied from a biographical rather than a cultural standpoint. Each piece of furniture described here is known to be the work of a specific cabinetmaker's shop, and included in each entry is a statement of its documentation. Documentation, as defined in this catalogue, may take the form of a signature, label, brand, or stamp; it may be derived from a surviving bill or ledger entry; or it may utilize a combination of these types of evidence.

Furthermore, only those pieces which bear the names (and in some cases the handwriting) of men known to have been cabinetmakers have been included. While many pieces of New Hampshire furniture have signatures, brands, stamps, or similar markings, not all—in fact, not many —of the names are those of makers. In a recent study of names branded on Portsmouth furniture (Myrna Kaye, "Marked Portsmouth Furniture," *Antiques*, May 1978, pp. 1098–1104), none was found to be that of a cabinetmaker. Numerous pieces of marked furniture were examined during the preparation of this catalogue; in relatively few cases did deed and probate searches, tax lists, and newspaper and genealogical research reveal that the names were those those of cabintmakers.

No furniture has been included that is merely attributed to a craftsman, no matter how well founded that attribution might appear to be or how generally accepted it may have become. This rather restrictive approach is not meant to deny the importance of attribution. On the contrary, the documentation provided in this catalogue should permit an increasing reliability in future attributions by recording examples of New Hampshire furniture known to have been made by a specific man in a specific place at a specific time.

It is ironic that the best known and most thoroughly studied examples of New Hampshire furniture are those associated with John and Samuel Dunlap, very few of which can be accurately dated, assigned to a particular maker, or traced to an original owner despite the thorough research of Charles S. Parsons (*The Dunlaps and Their Furniture* [Manchester, N.H.: The Currier Gallery of Art, 1970]). The work of the Dunlaps is a notable and interesting exception to the rule that New Hampshire furniture displays no specifically regional characteristics. The distinctive and highly inventive stylistic features of Dunlap furniture were first noted in the 1920s, during the earliest period of the study of American cabinetwork. The strongly regional traits of Dunlap furniture allowed researchers to identify, first, the origin of that furniture in the Merrimack Valley, and, ultimately, the identity of the family that made these unusual pieces.

The furniture of John Dunlap and his younger brother Samuel appears to derive from a combination of circumstances that were peculiar to the central part of the state before 1800 but seem to have disappeared as the Federal style swept through New Hampshire. Dunlap furniture represents the convergence of two traditions: the ornamental style of the Merrimack Valley as interpreted and embellished by men of Scottish heritage, and the academic style of the seacoast. It may be that only in the work of the Dunlaps did such a synthesis occur in New Hampshire. The process could probably have taken place only in towns that had retained a decorative heritage from the seventeenth or early eighteenth century, and yet were exposed to the more cosmopolitan styles of the coast. Moreover, such a synthesis could probably have occurred only in a limited time period, when public demand for the newest Federal fashions, based on patterns from large cities, had not yet thrown the native decorative style into disrepute. The work of John Dunlap's son, occurring after the advent of the Federal style, shows few of the distinctive family traits.

While Dunlap furniture can be recognized and associated with a specific family, other groups of New Hampshire furniture have been identified but not yet attributed to particular makers. The first group was recognized in 1965, when M. Ada Young published an article ("Five Secretaries and the Cogswells," *Antiques*, October 1965, pp. 478–485) in which she discussed five desks and bookcases and two chests of drawers with a number of shared characteristics. Since that time at least one desk and one chest of drawers have been added to the group. All have serpentine fronts and ogee bracket or claw-and-ball feet. The desks and bookcases vary in style—some having flat cornices and others having broken scrolled pediments with urn-and-flame finials—but the pieces share enough characteristics to suggest that they are the product of a single master craftsman. While Mrs. Young associated the group with a member of the Cogswell cabinetmaking family of Massachusetts, it now appears that the furniture was made about 1800 in the Gilmanton area by a still-unidentified craftsman.

A second group of desks and bookcases, also dating from about 1800 and probably originating in the Exeter-Kingston area, is similarly characterized by serpentine fronts, claw-and-ball feet, and broken scrolled pediments. Despite their shared features, differences between the Gilmanton and Exeter groups are sufficient to indicate separate makers. While family tradition ascribes one of the Exeter desks and bookcases to General Enoch Poor (who is said to have been apprenticed as a cabinetmaker), Poor's death some twenty years before this piece was made indicates that credit for this fine group of pieces belongs to a cabinetmaker whose identity is not yet known.

While the furniture of the Dunlaps and the anonymous Gilmanton and Exeter makers has certain stylistic hallmarks, visible similarities do not always link pieces by the same maker. Men trained or employed in urban shops appear to have regarded the ability to produce diverse cabinetwares as proof of mastery in their trade. A sophisticated cabinet-maker had such a wide range of techniques and materials at his command that he could easily fashion pieces with few (if any) stylistic similarities. The wide variety of furniture by Langley Boardman and Judkins and Senter of Portsmouth, which has been identified through ledger entries and bills, illustrates this fact, as do the seemingly unrelated birch desk and veneered bureau signed by Ephraim Mallard of Gilmanton. The highly-developed skills of trained cabinetmakers may have helped erase the traces of a personal style. Furthermore, the furniture in this catalogue does not necessarily represent the full range of forms or styles which each man was capable of producing. In several instances limitations of space have required that a cabinetmaker be represented by a piece that seems to embody his best work, and that known examples of a less ambitious nature be omitted.

Many New Hampshire cabinetmakers were eager to convince their potential customers that they owned, and would faithfully copy, the latest "patterns". In 1808 Levi Bartlett of Concord informed "his Customers and friends, that he has lately received from the first Furniture Ware-Houses in New-York and Boston, the latest London and Paris Patterns for Cabinet Furniture, by which he will Manufacture and Ornament to any taste which can be desired." A year later Porter Blanchard, who had bought Bartlett's business, advertised "the most modern Boston patterns," while John Ladd, one of Blanchard's competitors, noted that he had "just received the latest patterns from Boston and New-York, for CABINET WORK, which he flatters himself that he can execute and ornament to any persons taste." When Bliss and Horswill established their partnership in Charlestown, they specifically promised that their work would be done "with as much neatness as at Philadelphia, Newyork, Boston, or any other sea port." Clearly, the purpose of such advertising was to reassure the rural New Hampshire customer that furniture purchased from a local cabinetmaker would not appear naïve by comparison with examples from elsewhere.

Given the diligence of New Hampshire cabinetmakers in obtaining the latest urban patterns and the evident preference of customers for pieces made from such designs, it is not surprising that much of the state's furniture bears a strong resemblance to that of the larger coastal cities. The exact nature of the patterns that local craftsmen obtained from New York or Boston, is, however, unknown. While several cabinetmakers' price books were published in New York and other cities, none is yet known from Boston; none from any American city, as far as can be determined, would have been sufficiently well illustrated to convey accurately the subtle details of local style. Yet detailed patterns must have been available in some form; Porter Blanchard's furniture for the New Hampshire State House, to cite one example, is so close to Boston prototypes that it has long been attributed to that city.

Many discoveries in New Hampshire cabinetmaking await future researchers. A number of the state's largest towns are known to have supported their predictable share of cabinetmakers, yet no example of documented furniture from these communities has yet come to light. This is true of towns in the Connecticut Valley (which collectively had a population of about 43,000 by 1800), and particularly the more northerly towns in both the Connecticut and Merrimack valleys. Current research by Charles S. Parsons has identified seven cabinetmakers working before 1825 in Walpole, seven in Charlestown, two in Hanover, five in Haverhill, three in Littleton, two in Lancaster, and two in Plymouth. With the exception of the two pieces in this catalogue by Bliss and Horswill of Charlestown and the single example by Michael Carleton of Haverhill, documented furniture by these northern cabinetmakers has not been located. Occasionally, towns in the central or southern parts of the state have been equally unyielding. At least fourteen cabinetmakers worked in Sanbornton before 1825, and the seacoast towns of Exeter and Stratham supported twenty-two or more; none of their products has come to light. Similarly, the furniture of Abel Wilder, Abijah Wilder, Abijah Wilder, Jr., and Azel Wilder, all of Keene, has not been identified despite the Wilders' many newspaper advertisements testifying to the variety and quantity of their cabinetwork. Finally, relatively few pieces of furniture dating from before 1800 have been found. Although the tendency for cabinetmakers to sign or label furniture seems to have been sporadic and weak before the end of the eighteenth century, there are undoubtedly examples yet to be discovered.

This catalogue, like others of years past, represents one step forward in the continuing process of defining New Hampshire's material culture. Cabinetwork, like any other human artifact, is an expression of the skills and aesthetics of its creator and of the needs and fashions of the society in which he works. It is hoped that the firm evidence presented here will lead to a new sophistication in understanding New Hampshire cabinetwork and society during the pre-industrial era.

*James L. Garvin*
CURATOR

# Catalogue

# The Piscataqua Region

## 1 Side Chair, 1802

DOCUMENTATION: Entry of 13 September 1802 in Ledger B of Portsmouth merchant James Rundlet, noting the purchase of "8 mahogany Chairs" for $68 from Langley Boardman.

This chair, one of a set of six side and two armchairs, differs considerably from examples usually associated with Portsmouth cabinetmaker Langley Boardman, sharing with them only the use of tapered and molded front legs. Like most pieces of furniture made by or attributed to Boardman, however, the chairs reveal strong Salem characteristics. The curved cresting rail and thin splats with water-leaf terminals, in particular, are seen in several sets of chairs with Salem histories; the molded front legs, which have been regarded as characteristic of Boardman chairs, likewise occur in many Salem examples. These strong Essex County features are explained by Boardman's birth in Ipswich and his presumed Salem-area training, as well as by his continuing contacts in that vicinity.

The chairs that have been most frequently associated with Boardman have square backs with reeded stiles and rails, and carved corner rosettes. One such set was retained in the Boardman house until about 1900 by descendants of the cabinetmaker. The existence of the Rundlet set, made in the early years of Boardman's Portsmouth career, establishes his mastery of a type of chair not previously associated with his shop.

WOODS: mahogany; secondary wood (where visible), birch.

DIMENSIONS: H. 37½ in. (95.3 cm.)  W. 20⅜ in. (51.7 cm.)  D. 20¾ in. (52.6 cm.)

Lent by the Society for the Preservation of New England Antiquities, Rundlet-May House

## 2 Chest of Drawers, 1802

DOCUMENTATION:    Entry of 6 May 1802 in Ledger B of Portsmouth merchant
James Rundlet, noting the purchase of a "Beaureau & handles" for $28
from Langley Boardman.

This chest of drawers, with its exaggerated serpentine front, flared sides,
canted front corners, and brass "handles" on each end, relates to a small
group of Portsmouth chests, one of which has traditionally been attributed
to Boardman. This is the most sophisticated of the group; its refinements
of form and inlaid decoration are reflected in the original price which was
higher than that of a mahogany bedstead and twice that of a pembroke
table made for Rundlet at about the same time.

 The chest reveals the cabinetmaker's strong Salem heritage. A similar
piece, lacking the inlay and outswept corners of the Boardman example,
was made by Thomas Needham of Salem. Boardman used stringing to
outline the bracket feet, canted corners and drawer fronts of his chest; a
corresponding technique was used on labeled Salem pieces as well as
others made elsewhere in Massachusetts and Rhode Island.

WOODS:    mahogany and mahogany veneers with light and dark wood inlays; secondary woods, mahogany and pine.

DIMENSIONS:    H. 36 in. (91.4 cm.)   W. 43¼ in. (109.8 cm.)   D. 23¼ in. (59.0 cm.)

Lent by the Society for the Preservation of New England Antiquities,
Rundlet-May House

# 3  Lolling Chair, 1803

DOCUMENTATION:  Entry of 10 December 1803 in Ledger B of Portsmouth merchant James Rundlet, noting the purchase of a "Lolling chair" for $8 from Langley Boardman.

In contrast to the easy chair, which was used in the bedchamber, the lolling or "Martha Washington" chair commonly occurs in inventory listings for the parlor. Lolling chairs were a favorite form in Federal New England, possibly because they were relatively inexpensive. This chair cost Rundlet the same amount as one of Boardman's carved mahogany side chairs, and less than an armchair in the same set. Several upholsterers are known to have been working in Portsmouth at the time this chair was made; Boardman may have employed one in his own shop, since he advertised lolling and easy chairs as early as 1799.

Among the distinguishing features of the chair are the rounded juncture of arm and arm support, the flaring "ears" of the back (a structural feature, not an effect gained in upholstering), and stringing that extends to the end of the leg without a cuff. The design of the stringing at the bottom of the arm supports and the nature of the joint at the top of the front legs indicate that upholstery was intended to mask this area.

WOODS:  mahogany with light wood inlays; secondary wood (where visible), birch.

DIMENSIONS:  H. 43⅛ in. (109.5 cm.)  W. 24⅞ in. (63.2 cm.)  D. 38 in. (96.5 cm.)

Lent by the Society for the Preservation of New England Antiquities, Rundlet-May House

27

## 4 Night Table (Commode), 1803

DOCUMENTATION: Entry of 16 February 1803 in Ledger B of Portsmouth merchant James Rundlet, noting the purchase of a "Night Table" for $14 from Langley Boardman.

Boardman's use of the phrase "Night Table" to describe a rather expensive piece of furniture is puzzling until one consults Thomas Sheraton's *The Cabinet Dictionary*, where the form is defined as "a useful piece of furniture for night occasions." There is ample evidence that American cabinetmakers employed Sheraton's term for a commode or close stool; for example, the best chamber of the Peirce mansion in Portsmouth, when inventoried in 1814, contained "1 Mahogany Night Table & Pan." Boardman and two other Portsmouth cabinetmakers, itemizing the estate of William Senter in 1827, listed one night table in his house and three more in the Judkins and Senter shop.

Like other New England night tables of sophisticated design, this piece by Boardman is entirely deceptive in appearance. The cabinet doors, complete with brass keyhole escutcheons and triple stringing, are shams. The two drawers are actually a drop front hinged to the top, which in turn is hinged to the back of the piece and folds upward against the wall, revealing a commode seat.

WOODS: mahogany and mahogany veneers with light and dark wood inlays; secondary woods, birch, maple, and pine.

DIMENSIONS: H. 30⅞ in. (78.4 cm.)  W. 25¾ in. (65.4 cm.)  D. 18 in. (45.7 cm.)

Lent by the Society for the Preservation of New England Antiquities, Rundlet-May House

29

## 5 Side Chair, 1806

DOCUMENTATION: 1806 entry in Ledger B of Portsmouth merchant James Rundlet, noting the purchase of "6 fancy Chairs" for $24 from Josiah Folsom of Portsmouth.

This fancy chair is one of five which remain from the set of six purchased by Rundlet for his new house. The chairs share many characteristics with a second group in the Rundlet-May House and with others having Portsmouth histories. All have stiles that terminate in button finials, slender colonnettes decorated with ring turnings, curved seat frames, "cup" turnings at the top of the front legs, painted rosettes and quatrefoils at structural junctures, and striping in imitation of fluting. They are reminiscent of fancy chairs made in New York and Philadelphia, and in several cases the painted decoration relates closely to that on Baltimore seating furniture.

The Rundlet chairs of this set are painted off-white with gold, bronze, and brown decoration. Classical in inspiration, they are among the most elegant examples of American painted furniture of this period. Folsom is one of the few makers of fancy chairs whose work has been identified.

WOODS (where visible): mahogany and birch.

DIMENSIONS: H. 34⅜ in. (87.9 cm.)  W. 18 in. (45.8 cm.)  D. 19⅞ in. (50.5 cm.)

Lent by the Society for the Preservation of New England Antiquities, Rundlet-May House

## 6 Desk, 1812

DOCUMENTATION:  Manuscript bill dated 2 November 1812 from Judkins & Senter of Portsmouth to David Prebble for "Desk Mahog.y front & Birch ends 23.00".

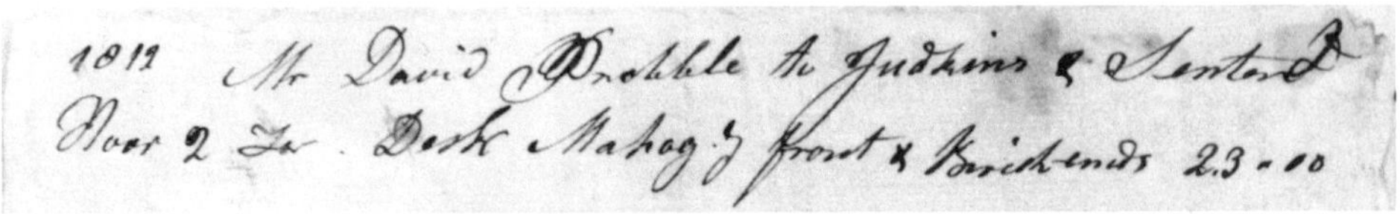

The existence of this desk, which has descended in the family of its original owner, provides evidence that the eighteenth-century slant-top form carried over into the Federal period. The visual separation of each drawer into three parts and the choice of veneers relate it to a large group of chests attributed to Portsmouth. Contrasting tones of crotch birch panels and mahogany cross-banding create a strong light-and-dark pattern which has come to be considered typical of Portsmouth cabinetmaking in the early nineteenth century. In many bureaus from this area a "dropped panel" in the skirt echoes the panel of matched veneering at the center of each drawer.

Judkins and Senter charged a relatively high price for this piece, but it was still only about half the cost of a secretary and bookcase made for another customer at about the same time. As the bill shows, Prebble bartered yard goods and vegetables to cover almost the entire purchase price.

WOODS:  birch, and mahogany and birch veneers; secondary wood, pine.

DIMENSIONS:  H. 44⅛ in. (112.0 cm.)  W. 42⅜ in. (107.6 cm.)  D. 20⅞ in. (53.0 cm.)

Lent anonymously

32

## 7  Sideboard, 1815

DOCUMENTATION:   Manuscript bill from Judkins & Senter to Portsmouth merchant Jacob Wendell listing the sale of a "Side board" for $70 on 20 December 1815; entry of 1 January 1816 in Jacob Wendell's Ledger 2 (1814–27), noting "Cash pd. Side Board–$70–"; pencil inscription on bottom of upper right-hand drawer: "Made / & [  ] / January 22 / 1815 / by J & Senter".

This is the only piece of Portsmouth furniture now known that is signed and dated by its makers. A comparison of the penciled inscription with the dated bill of sale indicates that the sideboard was made nearly a year before it was purchased. Perhaps the piece had been sold previously and traded back to its makers; the side of the left-hand cabinet section is branded "J. HAVEN.", possibly for Joseph Haven whose house stood directly opposite Wendell's. Since Jacob Wendell himself traded a secretary to Judkins and Senter when he bought a more expensive one, it is evident that the firm did buy and resell used furniture.

Although darkened by time, the original composition of light and dark veneers in this sophisticated piece is still evident and striking. The edge of the top board and the upper sections of the legs are veneered in bird's-eye maple. The elliptical and rectangular panels on the drawer fronts of the central section are of well-matched figured birch; other panels and most cross-bands are mahogany, the panels being outlined with light wood stringing or simple inlaid bands.

WOODS:   mahogany and mahogany, maple, birch, and zebrawood(?) veneers with light and dark wood inlays; secondary woods, mahogany, birch, basswood, and pine.

DIMENSIONS:   H. 42¾ in. (108.4 cm.)   W. 70⅞ in. (179.3 cm.)   D. 23⅝ in. (59.8 cm.)

Lent anonymously

## 8  Side Chair, 1815

DOCUMENTATION:  Manuscript bill from Judkins & Senter to Portsmouth merchant Jacob Wendell listing the sale of a "Set of Chairs" for $28 on 20 December 1815; entry of 1 January 1816 in Jacob Wendell's Ledger 2 (1814–27) noting purchase of "½ doz Chairs @ 18/ 2 Arm Ditto @ 30/—$28".

One of the set noted in Judkins and Senter's 1815 bill, this side chair with its arched cresting rail, saddle seat, and effective use of stringing and carving represents a later (and less expensive) version of the chairs made in 1802 by Langley Boardman for James Rundlet. The Wendell set is in the Salem style that Boardman seems to have introduced to Portsmouth at the turn of the nineteenth century. Boardman relied upon molded or carved surfaces to achieve a delicately sculptured effect in dark mahogany; Judkins and Senter's use of broad, flat surfaces relieved by light stringing produces a very different result. The wide bands of inlay on each splat were apparently intended to represent the fluting on a column shaft, and the carving suggests the acanthus foliage of a Corinthian capital.

A pair of very similar chairs has been attributed to the Boston cabinetmakers John and Thomas Seymour. It is possible that they were actually the work of Judkins and Senter, or perhaps the Portsmouth cabinetmakers followed a Massachusetts prototype in fashioning this set, which has descended in the family of its original owner.

WOODS (where visible):  mahogany with light wood inlays.

DIMENSIONS:  H. 37⅜ in. (94.8 cm.)  W. 21½ in. (54.6 cm.)  D. 20⅞ in. (53.0 cm.)

Lent anonymously

## 9 Card Table, 1816

DOCUMENTATION: Manuscript bill from Judkins & Senter to Portsmouth merchant Jacob Wendell listing the sale of a "Sofa & Card Tables" for $70 on 7 June 1816; entry of 31 July 1816 in Wendell's Ledger 2 (1814–27), noting purchase of "1 pr. Card Tables & Sofa" for $70.

One of a pair of card tables that has descended in the family of the original owner, this piece utilizes dark woods instead of the maple and burl birch veneers often favored by Portsmouth-area cabinetmakers. Delicately turned legs with ebonized feet and a deliberately subdued coloration that results from the skillful combination of rosewood and figured mahogany veneers give these tables a dignified elegance. Another pair of card tables with almost identical legs but with inlaid birch skirts descended in the family of Portsmouth merchant James Rundlet, suggesting that Judkins and Senter made similar furniture forms in both light and dark coloration. The presence of three incised ellipses (evidently a sketch for an inlaid skirt design) on the pine rear rail of this piece suggests that additional variations were possible.

This table and its mate have certain features in common with other pieces purchased by Wendell from Judkins and Senter at about the same time. The outline of the swelled fronts and turreted corners of the tables is so like that of the central section of the sideboard (see no. 7) as to suggest that the same template was used for both forms. The unusual triple-turned cuff on the table legs is echoed on the sofa (see no. 10), though in other details the pieces are not markedly similar.

WOODS: mahogany and mahogany and rosewood veneers; secondary woods, birch and pine.

DIMENSIONS: H. 30⅛ in. (76.5 cm.) W. 38⅛ in. (96.8 cm.) D. 18½ in. (46.9 cm.)

Lent anonymously

38

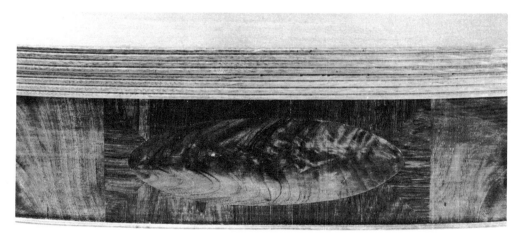

## 10 Square Sofa, 1816

DOCUMENTATION: Manuscript bill from Judkins & Senter to Portsmouth merchant Jacob Wendell listing the sale of a "Sofa & Card Tables" for $70 on 7 June 1816; entry of 31 July 1816 in Jacob Wendell's Ledger 2 (1814–27), noting purchase of "1 pr. Card Tables & Sofa" for $70.

Although purchased together, the sofa and card tables (no. 9) made by Judkins and Senter are not strikingly similar except in the turning of the feet and the use of reeding to add highlights to dark mahogany surfaces. The sofa lacks the light birch veneers and curved cresting rails seen on others with Portsmouth histories. However, the turned legs and "stumps" (arm supports) which merge into curved "elbows" (arms) relate closely to elements consistently noted in those sofas. A horizontally reeded cresting rail and incised rings on the legs and stumps give this sofa a later appearance than others attributed to Portsmouth, and may represent Judkins and Senter's attempt to update the traditional form. The sofa has descended in the family of its original owner.

WOODS: mahogany and mahogany veneers; secondary woods (where visible), oak and birch.

DIMENSIONS: H. 35½ in. (90.0 cm.) W. 73¾ in. (187.3 cm.) D. 28½ in. (72.4 cm.)

Lent anonymously

## 11  Side Chair, about 1845

DOCUMENTATION:  Brand on underside of seat, "A. F O L S O M & C°
D O V E R NH. / W A R R A N T E D".

This chair, like others in the set of six to which it belongs, may have been
made at Folsom's mill in East Rochester and decorated at his "Furniture,
Chair and Paint Store" in Dover. The variety of painted decoration—
which combines stenciling, freehand striping, rosewood graining, and
multicolored marbling—would seem to reflect the particular interest of
Folsom, who began his career as a portrait and ornamental painter. The
chairs of this set share with countless other mid-century chairs made
throughout the Northeast an urn-shaped splat, a plank seat with rolled
front edge, and a cresting rail with rounded ends and an undercut bottom.
The legs and stretchers are reminiscent of those used at the famous Hitchcock factory.

WOODS (where visible):  pine, birch.

DIMENSIONS:  H. 33⅜ in. (84.5 cm.)  W. 17¼ in. (43.7 cm.)  D. 16½ in.
(42.0 cm.)

New Hampshire Historical Society, Purchase

43

## 12  Side Chair, about 1850

DOCUMENTATION:  Stencil on underside of seat, "From / STEPHEN SHOREY, / CHAIRMAKER, / ROCHESTER, / N.H. / WARRANTED".

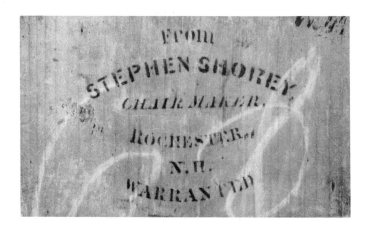

This chair, one of a pair, is perhaps typical of the three to four thousand chairs turned out each year at Shorey's Mills in East Rochester. The simplicity of the turned members of this example is in contrast to the complex elements used by Abraham Folsom (see no. 11), Shorey's predecessor at the same mill. The chairs are grained with red and black in imitation of rosewood, and the gilt floral stenciling on the cresting rail is complemented by freehand striping in yellow.

WOODS (where visible):   pine, birch.

DIMENSIONS:   H. 33½ in. (85.0 cm.)   W. 17⅞ in. (45.5 cm.)   D. 17 in. (43.1 cm.)

New Hampshire Historical Society, Purchase

45

# The Merrimack Valley

## 13   Desk, 1762

DOCUMENTATION:   Painted inscription on outer surface of backboards, "February / 23.d 1762. / John Kimball."

This desk is the earliest piece of documented New Hampshire furniture presently known. It descended in the family of General John Stark and his wife, Elizabeth Page, who were married in 1758 and lived in Derryfield (now Manchester). The maker, John Kimball, was born in Bradford, Massachusetts, and evidently worked in Derryfield before settling permanently in Concord by 1764.

The desk is tall and narrow in proportion and of sturdy construction. The interior reveals Kimball's inventiveness and skill; utilizing a combination of projecting, receding, convex, and concave elements, it resembles the finest mid-eighteenth-century Boston pieces. Behind this artful facade are a variety of ingeniously-contrived secret compartments. While the desk is clearly the work of a country joiner, it derives its inspiration from sophisticated Massachusetts examples.

WOODS:   maple; secondary wood, pine.

DIMENSIONS:   H. 43⅞ in. (111.5 cm.)   W. 35½ in. (90.1 cm.)   D. 18⅞ in. (48.0 cm.)

New Hampshire Historical Society, Purchase

46

## 14 High Chest of Drawers, 1762

DOCUMENTATION: Painted inscription on outer surface of backboards, "Deryfield / May ye 26. / 1762. / John Kim'l."

This high chest was made by Kimball for the John Stark family of Derry-field, now Manchester. Together with a desk made in the same year (no. 13), it provides evidence that Kimball, a prominent Concord joiner, worked briefly in Derryfield on his way up the Merrimack Valley from his birthplace in Essex County, Massachusetts. The signatures on these pieces are identical to those on documents which Kimball later signed in Concord.

Both the desk and the high chest are tall and narrow in proportion and have secret drawers and identical brass hardware. Dovetails that extend beyond the backs of the drawers are an unusual shared feature. Although the deeply-cut skirt of the high chest may appear to presage the inventiveness of the Dunlap school, the piece is actually far closer to Massachusetts prototypes. The use of attenuated and nearly vertical legs, a bottom section shallow in height, and mouldings based on classical profiles are strongly reminiscent of Boston, Charlestown, and Salem furniture of the mid-eighteenth century.

WOODS: maple; secondary wood, pine.

DIMENSIONS: H. 75⅝ in. (191.2 cm.) W. 38½ in. (97.7 cm.) D. 20¾ in. (52.6 cm.)

Lent by the Manchester Historic Association

49

## * 15   High Chest of Drawers, 1780

DOCUMENTATION: Chalked signature on bottom board of top section, "Will^m Houston".

Despite the prolific furniture production revealed by the surviving account books of John and Samuel Dunlap, few pieces can be documented to the shop of either man. This high chest of drawers bears the chalked signature of William Houston, who was apprenticed to John Dunlap between March 1775 and July 1776; it thus appears to be a product of Dunlap's Bedford shop. Also chalked inside the chest is the name "Miller" and the date "1780". Although Houston bought land in Peterborough in 1779, he witnessed an indenture in John Dunlap's shop in 1785. Thus, Houston seems to have worked intermittently for his old master and may have been employed on this piece in 1780.

The chest displays most of the forms associated with Dunlap furniture, including the "basket-weave" cornice, "flowered O G" crown moulding, carved shells of various designs, and moulded S-scrolls on the skirt.

WOODS: maple; secondary wood, pine.

DIMENSIONS: H. 83¼ in. (211.5 cm.) W. 41⅞ in. (105.5 cm.) D. 20¾ in. (53.2 cm.)

Courtesy of The Henry Francis du Pont Winterthur Museum

## 16 Tall Clock, 1792

DOCUMENTATION: Handwritten paper label on inner surface of backboard, "Ebenr Virgin / Of Concord / March 17th 1792—".

Except in the design of its base, this monumental tall clock is closely related to four clock cases labeled by Hopkinton joiner David Young and a virtually identical labeled case by Asa Kimball (see no. 18) of Concord, who was related to Young. Ebenezer Virgin had associations in Hopkinton, and is known to have married there.

Virgin's impressively tall case differs in minor details from that of Young (see no. 32). It should be noted, however, that the Young clock shown here is unusual among his labeled cases for its small proportions. The base of the clock by Virgin is unlike any known Young or Kimball example, but is somewhat related to one labeled by Moses Hazen of Weare. The pronounced curve of the ogee bracket feet, the intricate lower outline of the case, and the use of more than one type of decorative fan are reminiscent of work associated with the nearby Dunlap circle, but also occur in other rural sections of New England.

WOODS: cherry, birch, and maple; secondary wood, pine.

DIMENSIONS: H. 96½ in. (245.1 cm.) W. 22¼ in. (56.5 cm.) D. 12¼ in. (31.1 cm.)

Lent anonymously

DOCUMENTATION:   Printed paper label on outer back rail, "M A D E / B Y / Choate & Martin, / Concord, / New Hampshire."

Between 1794 and 1796 Robert Choate and George W. Martin advertised in Concord newspapers as a cabinetmaking and chairmaking partnership. Both men apparently came to Concord from Essex County, Massachusetts, —Choate having been born in Newburyport, Martin probably in Marblehead.

This circular card table is the only labeled product of their shop known to survive today. Its tapered legs are bordered with light line stringing which, instead of terminating at cuffs, extends to the floor in a manner associated with eastern Massachusetts craftsmanship. This feature was carried by migrating Massachusetts cabinetmakers not only to Concord, but also to Portland, Maine, where it is associated with the work of Benjamin Radford, who was born in Marblehead and trained in Salem.

WOODS:   mahogany and mahogany veneers with light and dark wood inlays; secondary woods, pine and birch.

DIMENSIONS:   H. 28¾ in. (73.0 cm.)  W. 35⅞ in. (91.0 cm.)  D. 17¾ in. (45.0 cm.)

New Hampshire Historical Society, Purchase

55

DOCUMENTATION:   Printed paper label on inner surface of backboard, "MADE / BY / Asa  Kimball, / CABINET  &  CHAIR / MAKER, / Concord, New Hampshire."

The case of this tall clock, labeled by Concord cabinetmaker Asa Kimball, is of a type made throughout New England by the late eighteenth century. Labeled cases of almost identical design can be found from as far away as Newport, Rhode Island. The style apparently originated in Roxbury, Massachusetts, appearing in its original form in the work of the famous Willard clockmaking family. Some of the features which tall clocks of the early "Roxbury" type share are ogee bracket feet, engaged quarter columns with brass cabling, arched cornices, open fretwork crests of a particular pattern, and brass finials.

Clock cases labeled by George W. Rogers of Concord, Moses Hazen of Weare, and William Rogers of Hopkinton differ from Asa Kimball's work only in minor details. This design seems to have been especially popular in the Concord area. No less than eight tall clocks of the same general type have movements by Timothy Chandler, who made the brass eight-day movement in this example.

WOODS:   mahogany and mahogany veneers; secondary wood, pine.

DIMENSIONS:   H. 90¾ in. (230.5 cm.)   W. 20¼ in. (51.3 cm.)   D. 10⅞ in. (27.6 cm.)

Lent anonymously

57

DOCUMENTATION:   Fragment of printed paper label in drawer, "GEORGE
  W. RO[GERS]".

In a pioneering article on New Hampshire cabinetmakers published in
*American Collector* (June 1937), Paul H. Burroughs identified the fragmentary label on this desk and bookcase as that of George W. Rogers of
Concord. Rogers came to Concord from Newburyport, Massachusetts,
about 1800. Because of the desk's unique combination of characteristics,
there is little doubt that he was the maker.

   Certain features of this piece that are associated with Newburyport
cabinetwork are also found in the Concord area, perhaps due to Rogers'
migration. Inlaid broken pilasters almost identical to those flanking the
cabinet section of this desk appear on a clock case of Newburyport manufacture; five pieces with this type of decoration, which does not seem to
have been common throughout New Hampshire, have definite associations with the Concord area. The interlaced pattern of stringing on the
frieze of this piece appears on several secretaries labeled by Salem cabinetmakers. Spade feet, although uncommon in New England, are found on
some fine Boston and Salem furniture. One unusual detail without known
parallel in the Newburyport area is the desk's inverted bellflower inlay,
which also occurs on the case of a clock by Abel Hutchins of Concord.

WOODS:   mahogany and mahogany and birch veneers with light wood inlays;
  secondary wood, pine.

DIMENSIONS:   H. 53½ in. (135.9 cm.)   W. 41½ in. (105.4 cm.)   D. 19⅞ in.
  (50.5 cm.)

Courtesy of Mrs. John D. Wright

59

DOCUMENTATION:   Printed paper label on outer surface of backboard, "House Furniture. / Cabinet work, Chairs, Clocks, and Time- / pieces of all kinds, and the latest fashions, / sold one door north of Mr. B. Gales Tav- / ern in Concord, N.H. and warranted good / BY LEVI BARTLETT."

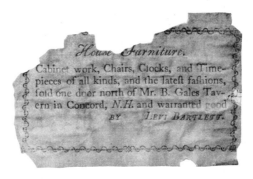

In 1805 Levi Bartlett advertised that he was taking over the Concord cabinet shop of Hubbard C. Gale, who had recently died and for whom Bartlett had worked. This chest of drawers, labeled by Bartlett, is similar in form and decoration to one bearing Gale's label dated 1804. Although the Gale chest was included in the Currier Gallery's 1964 exhibition of New Hampshire decorative arts, its present location is not known. Both chests have an inlaid band along the bottom of the case, a simply curved skirt with a small inlaid fan at its center, and French feet without spur brackets. This combination of features, frequently seen on Concord-Hopkinton–area case pieces, was apparently not common elsewhere.

Bartlett's address, given on the label as "one door north of Mr. B. Gales Tavern," dates this piece between 1805 and 1808; in the latter year Bartlett moved his shop to a new location.

WOODS:   mahogany veneers with maple and light wood inlays; secondary wood, pine.

DIMENSIONS:   H. 37 in. (94.0 cm.)   W. 41 in. (104.0 cm.)   D. 22¼ in. (56.5 cm.)

Lent anonymously

## 21 Card Table, 1808–1809

DOCUMENTATION: Printed paper label on inner back rail, "Mahogany, Cherry, and / Birch Furniture, of all / kinds, and of the latest / fashions, manufactured / BY LEVI BARTLETT, / opposite Gal[e]'[s] Tavern, / Concord, N.H."

A variety of inlays and veneers in striking combination give this card table by Levi Bartlett of Concord distinction. The elaborate broken pilaster design, although generally associated with Boston and Newburyport, Massachusetts, appears on several pieces from the Concord vicinity. Bartlett's version of the broken pilaster, however, differs in scale and execution from those on a Concord desk and bookcase by George W. Rogers, also described in this catalogue (see no. 19). It is possible that the relatively fine quality of Bartlett's inlaid borders and pilasters is due to his effective combination of plain and patterned bands made by inlay specialists and purchased by the cabinetmaker ready-made. When Bartlett advertised the stock from his cabinet shop for sale in 1811, he listed as available for purchase "English String and Banding."

This piece dates from the end of Bartlett's short but apparently productive career as a cabinetmaker. It was not until 1808 that his shop was located "opposite Gale's Tavern," as described on this label. The following year Bartlett sold his business to Porter Blanchard.

WOODS: mahogany and mahogany, rosewood, and satinwood veneers with multi-colored inlays; secondary woods, pine and birch.

DIMENSIONS: H. 28⅜ in. (72.0 cm.) W. 35¾ in. (90.7 cm.) D. 17½ in. (44.5 cm.)

Lent by Dwight E. Robinson and Lucy Grosvenor Robinson

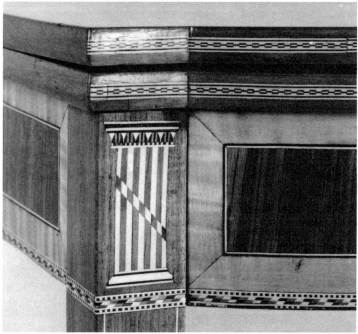

## 22 Desk, about 1810

DOCUMENTATION: Ink inscription on small interior drawer, "Ephraim Mallard".

Several cabinetmakers are known to have worked in the Gilmanton area, and an important group of late-eighteenth-century desks and bookcases is associated with that town. Although the name of James Chase is one which has been tentatively linked with these pieces, Ephraim Mallard (who worked for Chase briefly) is the only Gilmanton cabinetmaker whose work has been identified. There are no significant similarities between this desk and the earlier Gilmanton pieces, although the arrangement of their interior compartments is somewhat related.

In addition to the maker's signature, the desk bears an inscription tracing its ownership to Major Napoleon Bonaparte Gale of Laconia. As Gale was born in 1815, it is likely that the original owners of the desk were his parents, Daniel and Abigail (Page) Gale, who were married in 1801 and lived in Gilmanton. Later the desk was owned on Eagle Island in Lake Winnipesaukee. One of the best-preserved examples of New Hampshire furniture, it retains traces of an original red stain. Its solid construction contrasts with the flamboyant veneering on Mallard's chest of drawers (no. 23), probably made about the same time.

WOODS:  birch; secondary woods, maple and pine.

DIMENSIONS:  H. 43 in. (109.1 cm.)  W. 40¼ in. (102.2 cm.)  D. 21 in. (53.2 cm.)

Lent by Daniel J. and Mary Frank Fox

DOCUMENTATION: Chalked inscriptions on backs of drawers and underside of top, "Ephraim" and "Ephraim Mallard".

Case pieces with veneered rectangular panels in the center of their skirts have been recognized as a distinctive type associated with the North Shore of Massachusetts and the Portsmouth area. This chest by Ephraim Mallard, skillfully made and veneered with choice woods, poses a number of questions regarding the geographical distribution of such "drop-panel" furniture. (See also no. 56.) Its sophisticated bowed front, delicate drawer inlays, and apparent date in the early 1800s suggest that Mallard may have been trained and employed in the Portsmouth area before beginning work in Gilmanton at the age of twenty-one. This possibility is strengthened by the fact that the chest descended in the family of Captain Thomas Thompson (1739–1809) of Portsmouth.

It may be, on the other hand, that the chest was made in Gilmanton and became associated with the Thompson descendants through marriage. The relatively wide overhang of the solid birch top and the rather straight French feet could indicate that the chest, like Mallard's birch desk (no. 22), is a country product.

WOODS: birch and birch, maple, and mahogany veneers with light and dark wood inlays; secondary woods, birch and pine.

DIMENSIONS: H. 37⅞ in. (95.6 cm.) W. 40½ in. (102.9 cm.) D. 20¾ in. (52.7 cm.)

Private collection

## 24   Chest of Drawers, 1812

DOCUMENTATION:   Chalk inscription on outer surface of backboard, "S. Ross / Salisbury / September / 1812".

This chest of drawers, which relies for its elegant but subdued effect on a combination of rich mahogany veneers, finely executed inlays, and elaborate brasses, is unexpectedly sophisticated for the country town of Salisbury. It may, however, reflect the quality of craftsmanship in Gilmanton as well, for its maker, Stephen Ross, was the son of a Gilmanton cabinetmaker.

The drawer arrangement of this chest—in which three small drawers occupy the space of the long top drawer—is unusual in northern New England but found occasionally in Connecticut and New York. Ross's chest of drawers is in fact surprisingly similar, in drawer arrangement, depth of skirt, overall proportions, and subdued effect, to one made by Michael Allison of New York City about 1806. Advertisements prove that early-nineteenth-century New Hampshire cabinetmakers were definitely aware of design trends in major urban centers. Their advertisements in newspapers frequently mention having "just received the latest patterns from Boston" and sometimes also from New York.

WOODS:   birch, mahogany, and mahogany veneers with light and dark wood inlays; secondary wood, pine.

DIMENSIONS:   H. 38½ in. (97.8 cm.)   W. 40⅛ in. (101.9 cm.)   D. 22 in. (55.7 cm.)

New Hampshire Historical Society, Gift of the W. N. Banks Foundation

## 25  Circular Table, 1819

DOCUMENTATION:  Manuscript bill dated 1819 and headed "The State of New Hampshire to Porter Blanchard Dr. / for sundry articles of Furniture for the State House".

Desks or writing tables traditionally believed to have been part of the original furnishings of the New Hampshire State House have survived in both private and museum collections. On 25 June 1818 the legislature appropriated funds for the purchase of suitable furniture for the granite building then being erected. A recently-discovered bill itemizes twenty-seven pieces of State House furniture for which Concord cabinetmaker Porter Blanchard received payment in August 1819. This curved table and its mate, both in the New Hampshire Historical Society collections, are no doubt the "2 circular Tables" for the Senate Chamber for which Porter Blanchard was paid $70.

The provenance of the State House furniture has long been the subject of research and speculation. The surviving pieces were once attributed to eastern Massachusetts, their turnings and reeded decoration suggesting a Boston or Salem origin. Blanchard's advertisements help explain the similarity, for he promised that the furniture he made for his Concord patrons would be "in the newest fashions that the most modern Boston patterns will admit of".

WOODS:  maple, birch, and mahogany with maple veneers; secondary wood, pine.

DIMENSIONS:  H. 31⅞ in. (81.0 cm.)  W. 181½ in. (461.0 cm.)  D. 67 in. (170.2 cm.)

New Hampshire Historical Society, Gift of the State of New Hampshire

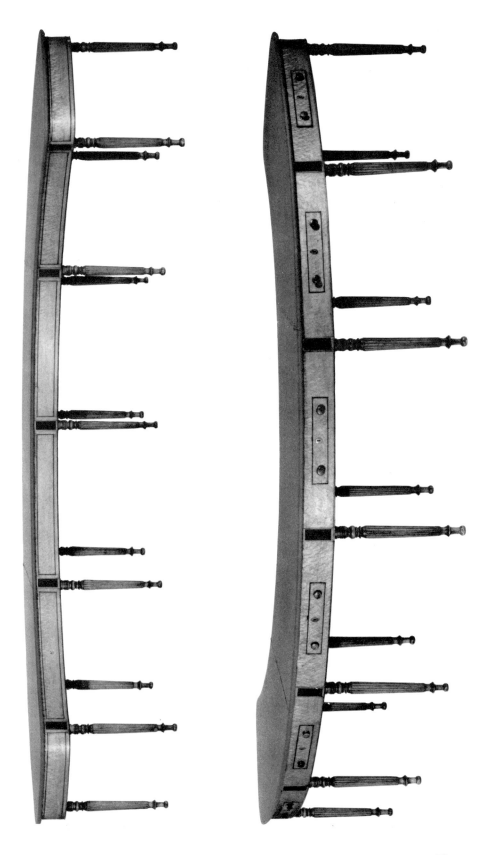

## 26  Desk, 1819

DOCUMENTATION:  Manuscript bill dated 1819 and headed "The State of New Hampshire to Porter Blanchard Dr. / for sundry articles of Furniture for the State House".

Desks and writing tables of several types (see no. 25) are listed on Porter Blanchard's bill for the New Hampshire State House furniture. This is one of two similar examples known to survive today; a third desk closely related to the other two is also extant. The fact that the desks were ordered for specific officials and chambers within the State House, as indicated on the bill, probably accounts for the variations among them. Despite their differences, Blanchard's State House pieces share a striking combination of elaborate form, colorfully-figured woods, and sturdy proportions. These characteristics, together with the use of such decorative details as the triglyphs on the skirt, have been noted on other furniture found in Concord or near Salisbury, where Blanchard had a second shop.

WOODS:  maple, birch, and mahogany with maple veneers; secondary wood, pine

DIMENSIONS:  H. 44 in. (111.7 cm.)  W. 60½ in. (153.5 cm.)  D. 31½ in. (80.0 cm.)

New Hampshire Historical Society, Gift of the State of New Hampshire

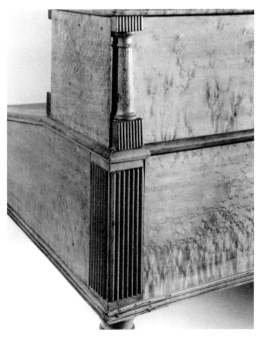

# 27  Armchair, 1819

DOCUMENTATION:  Manuscript bill dated 1819 and headed "The State of New Hampshire / To Low & Damon Dr".

This painted armchair is one of five known to survive from the original furnishings of the New Hampshire State House provided for in an appropriation of 1818. A recently-discovered bill has revealed the identity of the maker. On 3 February 1820, the Concord chairmaking and painting partnership of Low and Damon received payment from the State House Committee for one hundred eighty-two chairs of various types, together with eleven settees and three cushions.

The surviving chairs are an early, less common version of the institutional Windsors later made in great quantities by Hubbard and Haskell of Boston. In Low and Damon's chairs the imaginative interplay of convex, concave, and flat surfaces is accented by the use of black and yellow striping on an off-white ground. Decorative panels are grained in shades of brown. The center panel on the crest rail includes a representation of the New Hampshire state seal, incorporating a ship on the stocks and rising sun motif.

WOODS (where visible):   mahogany and birch; secondary wood, chestnut.

DIMENSIONS:  H. 36¼ in. (92.0 cm.)  W. 23½ in. (59.7 cm.)  D. 21¼ in. (54.0 cm.)

New Hampshire Historical Society, Gift of the State of New Hampshire

DOCUMENTATION:   Printed paper label in drawer, "ROBERT PARKER, / CABINET AND CHAIR MAKER, / BEDFORD, N.H."

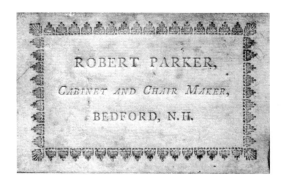

Born in Bedford in 1797, Parker established himself as an independent cabinetmaker there in 1819. He worked alone until 1823, when he formed a partnership with Jesse Richardson in Piscataquog Village, in north-eastern Bedford.

This chest is unusual for its artfully-curved swelled front and carved capitals on the reeded corner columns. The water-leaf carving and punched background of these capitals are reminiscent of Salem work at the same period. One other labeled chest by Parker, without carving, is known.

WOODS:   maple and cherry with mahogany veneers; secondary woods, maple and pine.

DIMENSIONS:   H. 48⅛ in. (122.3 cm.)   W. 43⅝ in. (110.8 cm.)   D. 21¾ in. (55.0 cm.)

New Hampshire Historical Society, Gift of the W. N. Banks Foundation

77

## 29 Side Chair, about 1830

DOCUMENTATION: Brand on underside of seat, "T. ATWOOD".

Thomas Atwood opened a chair factory in his native Bedford in 1819 after spending a number of years in Worcester, Massachusetts. During the 1830s he expanded his business to include cabinetmaking, and operated a furniture warehouse in Nashua. This example may be typical of the chairs he offered there "by the set or hundred". The use of bamboo turnings and arrow-shaped splats suggests earlier Windsor furniture.

WOODS (where visible): pine and birch.

DIMENSIONS: H. 34 in. (86.2 cm.)   W. 17 in. (43.0 cm.)   D. 18¾ in. (47.6 cm.)

New Hampshire Historical Society, Gift of Wilson Clyde

79

DOCUMENTATION:   Printed shipping label on outer surface of backboard,
"From / DANIEL A. HILL, / MANUFACTURER OF / CABINET
FURNITURE, / COUCHES AND LOOKING-GLASSES, / CON-
CORD, N.H."

A printed label addressed by hand to Edward P. Offutt, a Manchester
furniture dealer, identifies the maker of this chest as Daniel A. Hill of
Concord. In the Empire style and dating from about 1850, it is characterized by massiveness and simplicity relieved by the introduction of
scrolled surfaces. Another chest, dated 1850 and remarkably similar to this
one in form and proportion, bears the signature of James Bixby of
Francestown. Hill's first wife was probably from Deering (near Francestown) and had these pieces been made earlier, their similarity might have
suggested that Hill had been associated with cabinetmakers of that area.
However, because the chests are products of the mid-nineteenth century,
an era of greatly increased communications, further evidence is necessary
before this conclusion can be drawn.

WOODS:   maple with mahogany veneers; secondary woods, pine and maple.

DIMENSIONS:   H. 49⅞ in. (126.7 cm.)   W. 43⅛ in. (109.5 cm.)   D. 21 in.
(53.3 cm.)

Lent by Brenda Zinn Joziatis

## 31   Chest of Drawers, 1852–1854

DOCUMENTATION:   Stencil on outer surface of backboard, "FROM / A. P.
HOLMES. / No. 8 / Merrimack-Block / Manchester. / N.H[.]"

The fashion for "cottage furniture" began in the mid-1840s, and was
popularized in the writings of such men as Andrew Jackson Downing, the
landscape architect. Simple in form, this mass-produced chest is enlivened
by the use of bold, colorful swirls of painted decoration and graining. The
bulbous feet are also unusual. The maker of the chest, Andrew Paine
Holmes, was in business in Manchester for only two years.

WOODS (where visible):   pine; secondary wood, pine.

DIMENSIONS:   H. 31 in. (78.8 cm.)   W. 35 in. (88.8 cm.)   D. 15⅞ in. (40.2 cm.)

New Hampshire Historical Society, Purchase

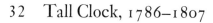

# The Contoocook and Souhegan Valleys

## 32  Tall Clock, 1786–1807

DOCUMENTATION:  Printed paper label on inner surface of backboard, "MADE / BY / David Young, / JOINER, / Hopkinton, Newhamp- / shire."

David Young probably produced many clock cases of this design, as at least four labeled examples are known: all house movements by Concord clockmakers. In this unusually short case, which is decorated with painted graining, is a movement by Levi and Abel Hutchins, brothers who worked together in Concord between 1786 and 1807.

Numerous unlabeled cases of this type are also known in the Concord-Hopkinton area. They share such features as wide proportions, high broken-scroll pediments, stylized pediment rosettes, brass urn finials, and identically-shaped bracket feet. The pediment scrolls of these clocks do not finish with a downward curve as do more sophisticated urban examples, but terminate abruptly at the highest point. It is perhaps significant that many of the same characteristics are found on cases made for Exeter and Kensington clockmakers, as Young is believed to have come from Kingston.

WOODS (where visible):  cherry, birch, and maple; secondary wood, pine.

DIMENSIONS:  H. 78 in. (198.1 cm.)  W. 21¾ in. (55.3 cm.)  D. 11¼ in. (28.5 cm.)

Lent anonymously

DOCUMENTATION: Printed paper label on inner surface of backboard, "MADE / BY / Moses Hazzen, / Joiner & Cabinet Maker, / New Hampshire."

Moses Hazen, Jr., lived in both Weare and Bradford, working as a joiner and cabinetmaker. He used several styles of printed labels for the various types of clock cases that he made.

This case is in the classic "Roxbury" style, which became popular in the Merrimack and Contoocook valleys. It is characterized by an arched hood with open fretwork and three brass finials, engaged quarter columns on the waist, freestanding colonnettes on the hood, and ogee bracket feet. Hazen used superbly-figured cherry for this example, adding stringing and an inlaid patera in the base. A similar case, unlabeled, is in the Society's collections.

WOODS: cherry and birch with light wood inlays; secondary wood, pine.

DIMENSIONS: H. 88⅛ in. (223.8 cm.)  W. 20¾ in. (52.6 cm.)  D. 10⅝ in. (27.0 cm.)

Lent by George L. Coombs

DOCUMENTATION: Printed paper label on inner surface of backboard, "James Dinsmore / CABINET [& CH]AIR / MAKE[R]"; "Hopkinton / N H" added below in ink.

This tall clock, a later version of the "Roxbury" type, is unusual because of the character of its inlaid decoration. The similarity between Dinsmore's inlay and that associated with John Dunlap II of Antrim suggests the existence of a regional inlay style shared by several cabinetmakers. Dunlap is said to have learned his trade from "a Mr. McAfee in Bedford," and Dinsmore may have had family associations in nearby Goffstown.

Although many features of this piece are not associated with the Hopkinton vicinity, the skirt with inlaid fan does relate to those on several case pieces by Hopkinton and Concord cabinetmakers. The pierced pattern of the crest is almost identical to that on a clock case labeled by Moses Hazen (see no. 33) of Weare, between Hopkinton and Goffstown. The fact that the unusual painted initials on the base are Dinsmore's own may be purely coincidental; if not, the case was perhaps made for his own use.

WOODS:    cherry with light and dark wood inlays; secondary wood, pine.

DIMENSIONS:   H. 91 in. (231.1 cm.)   W. 20¾ in. (52.6 cm.)   D. 10½ in. (26.5 cm.)

Lent by The Metropolitan Museum of Art, Rogers Fund, 1943

DOCUMENTATION:    Handwritten paper label on inner surface of backboard, "John Dunlap – 1807 / Cabinet and Chairmaker / Antrim".

This country-made tall clock boasts such refinements as fluted quarter columns on the waist and colonnettes on the hood. The distinctively-shaped fretwork is of a type frequently found on clock cases made in the Concord area; the two outer plinths and finials are missing.

The clock is grained, and painted in imitation of inlay. Dunlap simulated the appearance of dark inlaid banding by scoring the wood heavily and then applying stripes of black paint over the deep red ground. The use of painted decoration as well as carving and inlay (see nos. 36 and 46) suggests the range of this cabinetmaker's ability.

WOODS (where visible):    birch and maple; secondary wood, pine.

DIMENSIONS:    H. 85¾ in. (217.8 cm.)    W. 20⅝ in. (52.3 cm.)    D. 10½ in. (26.6 cm.)

Lent by Mr. and Mrs. A. H. Steenburgh

91

# 36 Card Table, about 1807

DOCUMENTATION:   Fragmentary handwritten paper label on underside of
top, "John Dunla[p]".

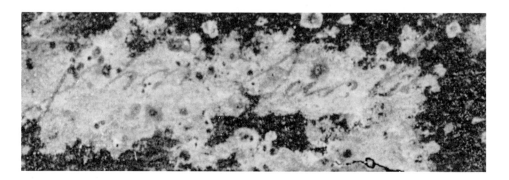

This example belongs to a group of tapered-leg card tables documented as
the work of John Dunlap II. All have rectangular panels outlined in light
wood stringing with engrailed ends on the skirt, and (on the upper legs)
intersecting arcs of stringing which terminate in dark inlaid bellflowers.
Two of the tables bear handwritten paper labels which read, "John Dunlap – 1807 / Cabinet and Chairmaker Antrim"; this card table is thought
to date from about the same time. It is unrestrained in its use of inlaid
decoration, displaying light and dark wood inlays, quarter fans, and
paterae. Particularly unusual are the circular motif seen on the top and
the foliate decoration that appears to have been burned into the inlaid
ovals on the stiles.

WOODS:   cherry and cherry veneers with light and dark wood inlays; secondary
woods, pine and birch.

DIMENSIONS:   H. 29⅜ in. (74.5 cm.)   W. 36 in. (91.4 cm.)   D. 17⅞ in. (45.3
cm.)

Lent by Dr. Benjamin A. Hewitt

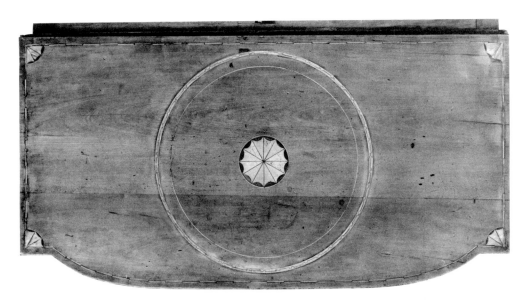

93

DOCUMENTATION: Printed paper label in drawer, "ALL KINDS OF / CABINET FURNITURE, / MADE AND SOLD BY / EPHRAIM BLANCHARD, / AMHERST, N.H."

This lady's desk and bookcase makes a restrained but eloquent statement about the quality of New Hampshire cabinetwork in the early Federal period. Its diminutive proportions and stylish appearance suggest that the maker was familiar with the fine cabinetwork then being produced in urban centers in his native Massachusetts. Relying for interest on delicate mouldings, careful veneering, and imaginatively designed muntins, Blanchard used dark wood inlay for contrast only at the cuffs of the legs.

A small inner drawer bears the pencil inscription "24 July 18 1811" in contemporary script. Although he is known to have worked in Amherst as early as 1803, most of Blanchard's surviving furniture is thought to date well after 1815.

WOODS:  mahogany and mahogany veneers with dark wood inlays; secondary wood, pine.

DIMENSIONS:  H. 58¼ in. (148.0 cm.)  W. 40 in. (101.7 cm.)  D. 21¼ in. (54.0 cm.)

Lent anonymously

DOCUMENTATION:   Chalk inscription on underside of top, "Oliver Batcheller / Cabinet maker".

The construction of this table, with its beveled top and sophisticated use
of veneers, reveals the fine craftsmanship of this New Ipswich maker.
Several elements of its design, especially the serpentine front, ovolo
corners, and bold combination of turnings and reeding on the legs and
corners, suggest tables made in Salem, Massachusetts, and may derive from
Batcheller's association (through his family) with nearby Marblehead. No
other furniture has been identified as the work of this maker, who died at
the age of twenty-five.

WOODS:   mahogany and mahogany, satinwood, and rosewood veneers with light
and dark wood inlays; secondary woods, birch and pine.

DIMENSIONS:   H. 30⅝ in. (77.7 cm.)   W. 38⅜ in. (97.5 cm.)   D. 18½ in.
(47.1 cm.)

Lent by Mr. and Mrs. Robert Taft

## 39  Breakfast Table, about 1820

DOCUMENTATION:   Printed paper label on underside of top, "ALL KINDS OF / CABINET FURNITURE, / MADE AND SOLD BY / EPHRAIM BLANCHARD, / AMHERST, N.H."

Although it lacks the delicacy that often characterizes the form, this pembroke or breakfast table does exhibit such refinements as rounded leaves, carefully turned and reeded legs, and diminutive brass casters.

Blanchard does not seem to have advertised in local newspapers before 1823, even though he was working in Amherst much earlier. In 1835 he offered "a general assortment of cabinet furniture", listing "Mahogany and Maple Tables" together with a wide variety of other items.

WOODS:   maple and birch; secondary wood, pine.

DIMENSIONS:   H. 28½ in. (72.4 cm.)  W. 37⅞ in. (95.3 cm.)  D. 18¾ in. (47.7 cm.)

New Hampshire Historical Society, Purchase

## 40 Chest of Drawers, about 1820

DOCUMENTATION: Printed paper label in drawer, "JOHN GOULD. Jr. / CABINET MAKER, / Near the Meetinghouse, in NEW- / IPS- WICH, manufactures in the / newest stile, all kinds [o]f / CHERRY & MAHOGANY FURNITURE. / Cash or Furniture [given for] / Cherry Boards and Plan[k]."

Exhibiting a high level of design and workmanship, this is one of a group of chests with flat or swelled fronts that have earned Gould a place at the forefront of his trade in New Hampshire. The chest is of simple but strong construction, attention having been given to every structural detail. It combines the styles and techniques of urban workmanship with a choice of woods generally preferred by country joiners. Gould's predilection for cherry, noted in his label, is demonstrated in this piece; the use of choice veneers of cherry over pine for the sides and drawer fronts suggests that the cabinetmaker considered cherry rare enough to be used frugally. The reeded corner columns and leg turnings are skillfully executed, and the ball feet retain traces of an ebonized treatment which is more pronounced on other pieces in this group.

WOODS: cherry and cherry and mahogany veneers with light and dark wood inlays; secondary woods, maple and pine.

DIMENSIONS: H. 39⅜ in. (99.9 cm.) W. 42⅜ in. (107.6 cm.) D. 22½ in. (57.2 cm.)

Lent anonymously

DOCUMENTATION:   Brand on underside of seat, "J. WILDER".

The work of Joseph Wilder of the prolific New Ipswich chairmaking family, this is one of a pair of chairs said to have been given for the chancel of a southwestern New Hampshire church dedicated in 1821. Freehand decoration in yellow, black, and white on a simulated tortoise-shell background includes—on the cresting rail—what appears to be a representation of the "two tables of stone" given to Moses on Mount Sinai.

With their mahogany arms, bamboo turnings, and "step-down" cresting rails, the chairs are similar to a group of side chairs stamped "WILDER" and presumed to be the work of either Joseph Wilder or his father, Peter. Other examples are known bearing Joseph Wilder's printed paper label; in at least one instance the label is pasted over the "WILDER" stamp.

WOODS (where visible):   pine and mahogany.

DIMENSIONS:   H. 36¼ in. (92.1 cm.)   W. 22⅜ in. (57.0 cm.)   D. 21⅛ in. (53.6 cm.)

Lent anonymously

103

# 42 Chest of Drawers, about 1825

DOCUMENTATION:   Fragment of printed paper label in drawer, presumably identical to that on desk and bookcase by the same maker, "[ALL KINDS OF / CABINET FURNITURE, / MADE AND SOLD BY / EPHRAIM BLANCHARD, / AMHERST, N.H.]"

This yellow painted chest, on which striping of orange bordered with reddish-brown appropriately takes the place of inlaid or applied embellishment, was evidently used in the cabinetmaker's own family. An affidavit, preserved by the lenders, states that it was "made and belonged to Ephraim Blanchard. His wife always expressed great affection for it in her declining years after leaving Amherst." The inventory of Blanchard's estate taken at the time of his death includes "1 Pine Bureau 4.50", which may be this chest. Of the surviving chests of drawers bearing Blanchard's label, only this one is made of painted pine; the others are of native hardwoods or of mahogany veneer over pine. Several have distinctive ovoid or "turnip" feet, and small dressing boxes are integral to all except one. Many of the chests also have freestanding colonnettes at the front corners.

WOODS (where visible):   pine and maple; secondary woods, pine and chestnut.

DIMENSIONS:   H. 45¾ in. (116.2 cm.)   W. 41⅝ in. (105.4 cm.)   D. 19½ in. (49.5 cm.)

Lent anonymously

## 43 Work Table, about 1825

DOCUMENTATION: Fragmentary printed paper label in drawer, identical to that on desk and bookcase by the same maker, "[ALL KINDS OF] / CABIN[ET FURNI]TURE, / MADE AND [SOLD BY] / EPH-[RAI]M BLAN[CHAR]D, / [AMHERST, N.H.]"

This sturdy table with its spiral-turned legs and drop leaves is typical of furniture made throughout New England in this period. The workmanship is that of a master craftsman. Shaped leaf supports, moulded side rails —visible only when the leaves are extended—and sham drawer faces on the back surface indicate that the table was carefully designed as a functional and decorative object.

Blanchard's career is more completely reprsented by surviving documented furniture than that of any other New Hampshire cabinetmaker. The five Blanchard pieces illustrated here (see also nos. 37, 39, 42, 49) range in date from about 1810 to about 1830 and express the successive styles of the period.

WOODS: mahogany and mahogany veneers; secondary woods, birch, maple, and pine.

DIMENSIONS: H. 28⅝ in. (72.6 cm.) W. 18½ in. (47.0 cm.) D. 18¼ in. (46.4 cm.)

Lent anonymously

## 44   Desk and Bookcase, about 1825

DOCUMENTATION:   Printed paper label (partly obscured by ink stain) on bottom board of bookcase section, "JOHN GOULD[.] J[r.] / CABI-NET MA[KER], / Near the Meeti[nghouse, in NEW-] / IPS-[WICH, manufactures in the / newest stile, all kinds of / CHERRY & MAHOGANY / FURNITURE. / Cash or Furniture given for / Cherry Boards and Plank.]"

In this desk and bookcase, John Gould demonstrated the same skill in veneering and turning that characterizes a group of bureaus (see no. 40) made in his shop. However, the somber coloration of this piece contrasts with the light-grained cherry veneers that Gould used on most of his chests. Large, complex, and undoubtedly expensive, the secretary has a dignified quality that results from the use of well-proportioned legs and columns, and dark veneers that contrast with brass hardware and bone keyhole escutcheons.

The vase-shaped columns and the reeded panels flanking the projecting upper drawers are highly reminiscent of similiar features in tables made by or attributed to Porter Blanchard of Concord. Blanchard's designs were often based on Boston patterns, so that it is difficult to say whether Gould was influenced more by Concord or Boston.

WOODS:   mahogany and mahogany veneers; secondary wood, pine.

DIMENSIONS:   H. 76 in. (193.0 cm.)   W. 40¼ in. (102.2 cm).   D. 21½ in. (54.5 cm.)

Lent by Mr. and Mrs. Warren E. Legsdin

## 45 Desk and Bookcase, about 1825

DOCUMENTATION: Pencil signature on shaped interior drawer, "Moses Osborn Esq".

Moses Osborn, Jr., the Quaker joiner who made this sturdy desk and bookcase, was working in Weare by the mid-1820s. In the fashion of much rural New Hampshire cabinetwork, it is made from a variety of native woods stained to a uniform reddish-brown. The unconventional shaping of the skirts and the use of a rather academic scrolled pediment stylistically unrelated to the base emphasize its "country" quality. The bookcase section is fitted with horizontal shelves and vertical dividers.

WOODS:   cherry, birch, and basswood; secondary woods, basswood and pine.

DIMENSIONS:   H. 75⅞ in. (192.0 cm.)   W. 39 in. (99.2 cm.)   D. 20 in. (50.8 cm.)

New Hampshire Historical Society, Gift of the W. N. Banks Foundation

III

## 46    Card Table, 1827

DOCUMENTATION:    Pencil inscription on underside of top, "John Dunlap /
Antrim May 30 / 1827".

This card table in the late Federal style is in marked contrast to an earlier
Dunlap example (see no. 36) which is characterized by the abundant use
of inlay. In this piece, leaf carving and a cross-and-punchwork ground on
the engaged colonnettes suggest a possible acquaintance with Salem, Massachusetts, cabinetwork. Dunlap's eccentric treatment of the legs—com-
bining spiral reeding and turned segments—is perhaps more suited to
another form, such as a chamber table.

WOODS:    mahogany and mahogany veneers; secondary woods, pine and birch.

DIMENSIONS (open):    H. 29½ in. (75.0 cm.)    W. 36⅛ in. (91.7 cm.)    D. 18⅛ in.
(46.1 cm.)

Lent by Mr. and Mrs. John W. F. Lloyd

DOCUMENTATION:   Handwritten paper label on underside of drawer, "No.
137 / Jeremiah Gooden / Cabinet Maker / Milford".

This two-drawer table is an example of the adaptation of a sophisticated
urban form by a country joiner. The delicate legs, which vary noticeably
in diameter, are marked at intervals by groups of incised lines that were
evidently inspired by the ring turnings seen in eastern Massachusetts
cabinetwork after 1800. Gooden may have used lines instead of rings because of his limitations as a turner.

   The table is simple but pleasing in design, and carefully executed.
The appearance of "No. 137" on the label suggests that Gooden was an
experienced craftsman who had already produced a considerable quantity
of furniture. A four-drawer pine chest bearing two of his handwritten
labels is also known.

WOODS:   maple and birch; secondary woods, chestnut and pine.

DIMENSIONS:   H. 26¾ in. (67.9 cm.)   W. 19¼ in. (48.8 cm.)   D. 19 in. (48.2
   cm.)

Lent by Rhoda Shaw Clark

DOCUMENTATION: Brand under seat, "A. WETHERBEE. / WAR-RANTED".

Although Wetherbee is referred to in the New Ipswich town history as a partner with his Wilder in-laws (Peter, Josiah Prescott, and John), he seems to have stamped with his own name the chairs he produced. This "Salem" rocker, with its scooped seat, bamboo turnings, and carefully-shaped spindles and arms is similar to one labeled by Minot Carter (see no. 50), another brother-in-law of J. P. Wilder. It is painted black with red graining, stenciled fruit and scroll decoration, and green and yellow striping.

WOODS (where visible):   birch and pine.

DIMENSIONS:   H. 43½ in. (110.5 cm.)   W. 23⅛ in. (58.6 cm.)   D. 22¼ in. (56.5 cm.)

Lent anonymously

## 49　Portable Desk, probably 1832

DOCUMENTATION:　Fragment of a letter from John Farmer to an unknown recipient, dated 1832, "Our friend, Mr. S. at Nashua, has lately sent me an elegant Portable desk, made by Mr. Blanchard, of Amherst, and I have written to him the first letter on it."

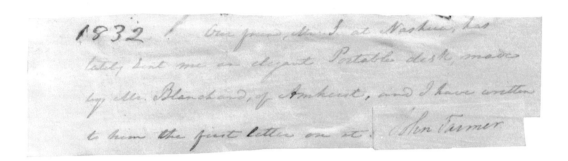

This brass-bound portable desk was presented to the Amherst Library in 1899, probably because of its association with John Farmer (1789–1838) of Amherst. Farmer was a founder of the New Hampshire Historical Society and its first corresponding secretary. A label affixed to the interior indicates that the desk was a gift to him from Isaac Spalding of Dunstable (Nashua). A useful accessory, it contains compartments for pens and other writing equipment as well as ample space for the storage of papers.

WOODS:　mahogany; secondary woods, mahogany and pine.

DIMENSIONS:　H. 6⅞ in. (17.4 cm.)　W. 20⅛ in. (51.0 cm.)　D. 10¾ in. (27.3 cm.)

Lent by the Historical Society of Amherst, New Hampshire, Inc.

Presented
to
John Farmer, Concord,
by his esteemed friend,
Isaac Spalding, Esq.
of
Dunstable, N.H.

DOCUMENTATION:   Printed paper label on underside of seat, "[WAR]-
RENTED  CHA[IRS]  /  MADE  BY  /  MINOT  CART[ER]  /  AT
WILDER'S  CHAIR  FACTO[RY,]  /  NEW-IPSWICH,  N.H.  /
Price $".

Minot Carter was related by marriage to Abijah Wetherbee and Josiah
Prescott Wilder, both of whom were also New Ipswich chairmakers.
Carter's interpretation of the "Salem" rocker differs only in minor details
from that of Wetherbee (see no. 48), and in fact carefully-bent back
spindles are characteristic of the rocking chairs made by all three men.
This example is painted in imitation of rosewood and decorated with yellow and now-faded salmon pink.

WOODS (where visible):   birch and pine.

DIMENSIONS:   H. 42¼ in. (107.2 cm.)   W. 22¾ in. (57.7 cm.)   D. 27⅜ in.
(69.5 cm.)

Lent anonymously

121

## 51  Side Chair, about 1847

DOCUMENTATION:  Brand on underside of seat, "J. P. WILDER / WAR-
RANTED".

According to his surviving account books, Josiah Prescott Wilder of New
Ipswich made a wide variety of chairs in quantity during the 1830s and
1840s. This example, one of a pair with freehand decoration in gold on a
black background, may be of the type Wilder described as "scroll seat
chairs" in an 1847 entry.

WOODS (where visible):  birch and pine.

DIMENSIONS:  H. 34¼ in. (87.0 cm.)  W. 17⅞ in. (44.8 cm.)  D. 18⅝ in.
(47.5 cm.)

New Hampshire Historical Society, Gift of Mrs. Donald K. Packard

123

# The Connecticut Valley

## * 52   Chest of Drawers, 1798

DOCUMENTATION:   Printed paper label in drawer, "Bliss and Horswill, / CABINET AND CHAIR MAKERS, / FROM BOSTON . . . / Charlestown, N.H. January 22, 1798."

Upon their arrival in Charlestown on the Connecticut River, Bliss and Horswill advertised as cabinetmakers "from Boston." This chest is evidence of their familiarity with Boston furniture construction and design. As on blockfront and bombé examples from that area, a deeply overhanging top is attached directly to the sides of the case without a space above the upper drawer. The omission of capitals on the columns may also relate to this eastern Massachusetts practice.

Fluted quarter columns are rarely found on Boston chests of this period; they were, however, relatively common in the Connecticut Valley. The use of brass bases for the columns is seen in furniture of the lower valley.

WOODS:   cherry; secondary wood, pine.

DIMENSIONS:   H. 35 in. (88.7 cm.)   W. 41⅛ in. (104.4 cm.)   D. 21 in. (53.5 cm.)

Courtesy of Mrs. Raymond F. Rickard

DOCUMENTATION: Printed paper label affixed to sacking on underside of seat, "Bliss and Horswill, / CABINET AND CHAIR MAKERS, / FROM BOSTON . . . / Charlestown, N.H. January 22, 1798."

This is one of the few pieces of American upholstered furniture on which a maker's label has survived. The location of the label—in a place where it could easily have loosened or been removed—helps explain its rarity.

Bliss and Horswill, who advertised not only that they made "Furniture of all kinds" including "Easy Chairs" but also that they would "stuff the same," probably also upholstered this piece. The sacking bears a pencil inscription (now concealed by upholstery) that reads: "8–12–14–98." If this refers to the date of manufacture, 12–14 August 1798, the chair may have been made by Thomas Bliss alone since John W. Horswill apparently left the partnership in June of that year.

Although the upholstery is modern, much of the original webbing and sacking is intact. Samples of the former tow stuffing also survive. The legs of the chair were pieced out following the removal of later casters.

WOODS: mahogany with light wood inlay; secondary woods, oak, maple, and pine.

DIMENSIONS: H. 47⅛ in. (119.7 cm.) W. 32¾ in. (83.2 cm.) D. 30¼ in. (76.8 cm.)

New Hampshire Historical Society, Gift of the W. N. Banks Foundation

DOCUMENTATION: Pencil inscription in drawer, "Eliphalet Briggs j / Keene January 9th 1810 / Made this $ 19 Doll."

Eliphalet Briggs, Jr., aged twenty-one, signed and dated this chest, perhaps as an example of his newly-acquired competence as a cabinetmaker. Although the flourish at the end of his name is not entirely legible, it appears frequently in the signature of the younger Eliphalet Briggs, and is known to stand for "Jr." A card table in the Mabel Brady Garvan Collection at Yale is signed "E Briggs" in what may be the same handwriting.

This chest of drawers is of a universally popular form inspired in part by published patterns that appeared in George Hepplewhite's *Cabinet-Maker and Upholster's Guide* and in *The Cabinet-Makers' London Book of Prices*. Examples believed to have been made in Connecticut, New York, and Philadelphia differ from Briggs' chest only in choice of woods and details of decoration. The brass handles bear the common but as-yet-unidentified English founder's mark "H·J" on the bail and are apparently original.

WOODS: cherry, and mahogany veneers with light and dark wood inlays; secondary wood, pine.

DIMENSIONS: H. 33½ in. (85.0 cm.) W. 41¾ in. (106.0 cm.) D. 22 in. (55.8 cm.)

Lent by Bertram K. and Nina Fletcher Little

DOCUMENTATION:   Stamp on top of swing leg and on underside of frame, "I. WILDER. j".

Once tentatively attributed to John Wilder of Keene, this table is now believed to have been made by Isaiah Wilder, Jr., who moved from Hingham, Massachusetts, to Surry, near Keene. After his removal to New Hampshire, Wilder seems not to have been referred to as "Jr.," but perhaps continued to use the same die.

A second table with the same stamp is owned by the New Hampshire Historical Society. It is similar in form, but of heavier proportions; instead of being grained, it is veneered with mahogany. Another table, identical in form but employing both birch and mahogany veneers, bears the stamp of an unidentified "T. GREEN." The general shape of these tables and the turnings of their legs are reminiscent of eastern Massachusetts examples.

WOODS (where visible):   pine; secondary woods, pine and maple.

DIMENSIONS:   H. 29¾ in. (75.5 cm.)   W. 35⅛ in. (89.2 cm.)   D. 17½ in. (44.3 cm.)

Lent by Old Sturbridge Village

## 56  Sideboard, about 1820

DOCUMENTATION:  Painted signature (partly obliterated) on underside of drawer, "[Mich]ael Carleton".

This sideboard appears to be virtually identical to one published in *American Collector* (June 1937) as the documented work of another Haverhill cabinetmaker, Stephen Adams (1778–1859). The present location of the piece, said to be dated 1810, is unknown, but its evident similarity to this example suggests a possible collaboration between Adams and Carleton.

The small sideboard is a form which seems to have found particular favor in New Hampshire. The proportions seen here are essentially those of a chest of drawers, with a deep top drawer and flanking bottle drawers instead of two long upper drawers. In this rural interpretation of a sophisticated furniture form, veneers and inlays have been successfully juxtaposed; the dropped panel—once thought to suggest a Portsmouth-area origin—is also present.

WOODS:  cherry and cherry, maple, mahogany, and birch veneers with light wood inlay; secondary wood, pine.

DIMENSIONS:  H. 38½ in. (97.8 cm.)  W. 43 in. (109.2 cm.)  D. 20½ in. (51.9 cm.)

Lent by Daniel J. and Mary Frank Fox

132

133

DOCUMENTATION:   Pencil inscriptions in drawer and on top of drawer divider, "Made by H Ellis / Newport N H" and "Horace Ellis, 1832".

This richly carved and veneered chest of drawers in the Empire style was originally owned by Dr. John Sabine Blanchard of Cornish who married Louisa Jackson in November of 1832. Horace Ellis, its maker, was the son of a local physician with whom Dr. Blanchard undoubtedly had professional associations.

Although Ellis did not have a long career in Newport, his work represents the fine craftsmanship of that cabinetmaking center. He is known to have been employed in the furniture shop of Willard Harris, in operation during the 1820s. The firm of Gilmore, Hall, & Dwinel, which bought the Harris business in 1831, pictured in their advertisements furniture similar to this chest. Since he did not advertise independently, it is possible that Ellis was working for this firm in 1832 when he made Blanchard's chest.

WOODS:   mahogany and mahogany veneers with light wood inlay; secondary woods, pine and basswood.

DIMENSIONS:   H. 57⅛ in. (145.0 cm.)   W. 47⅛ in. (119.6 cm.)   D. 22½ in. (57.0 cm.)

New Hampshire Historical Society, Purchase

# The Saco Valley

## * 58  Side Chair, about 1820

DOCUMENTATION:  Stamp on underside of seat, "J. R. HUNT / MAKER."

Although worn and stripped of its original red paint, this is the only known chair documented as the work of this maker which has bamboo-turned legs and back spindles. (The stretcher on the left side is a crude replacement.) Other chairs bearing Hunt's stamp are of the "thumb-back" and "step-down" types, frequently with bamboo-turned legs.

Probably trained in Boston, Hunt came to New Hampshire some-time after 1810. Like Elijah Stanton who worked in nearby Conway, he is identified in public records alternately as chairmaker and as cabinetmaker.

WOODS:  birch(?) and pine.

DIMENSIONS:  H. 33¾ in. (85.6 cm.)  W. 19 in. (48.1 cm.)  D. 17½ in. (44.3 cm.)

137

DOCUMENTATION:   Stencil on underside of seat, "E. STANTON . / . CON-WAY . / . N.H."

One of a set of six sturdily constructed half-spindle Windsors, this chair is grained in imitation of rosewood and has yellow striping. Stanton's version of the Windsor chair has a shaped plank seat which is thicker than most; another example with a different back design has recently come to light.

Although this set was found near Conway, the wording of Stanton's stenciled signature suggests that some of his chairs were sold elsewhere. Similar chairs were made throughout New England during the second quarter of the nineteenth century; many were local interpretations of the styles popularized by Lambert Hitchcock at his Connecticut chair factory.

WOODS (where visible):   maple and pine.

DIMENSIONS:   H. 33¼ in. (84.5 cm.)   W. 17⅛ in. (43.5 cm.)   D. 16¾ in. (42.5 cm.)

New Hampshire Historical Society, Purchase

# Biographical Sketches

ATWOOD, Thomas (1785?–1865)

Born in Bedford, Atwood married Susannah Holmes of Londonderry in 1808. The couple lived for several years in Worcester, Massachusetts, where four children were born between 1810 and 1817. Atwood is said to have returned to Bedford in 1819 and purchased a mill where he made furniture. He advertised in 1831 for "a good Workman at the CABINET BUSINESS." The following year the opening of a furniture warehouse in Nashua was announced by T. Atwood and son; "Flag bottomed, Fancy & Common CHAIRS, of all kinds, by the set or hundred" were offered. In May 1837 the firm of Atwood and Peabody was formed. Later that year Atwood advertised the sale of land in Merrimack and Bedford, and "at the subscriber's shop in Bedford . . . Secretaries, Bureaus, Mahogany Tables, Mahogany Work Stands, common Tables, Work Stands, Wash Stands, Bedsteads. . . ." In March 1840 his "Dwelling House, Barn, Saw and Grist Mills, and Cabinet Maker's shop" in Bedford were sold. He moved to Nunda, New York, and in 1860 to Canaseraga, New York, where he died.

BARTLETT, Levi (1784–1864)

Born on 3 June 1784 in Salisbury, Levi was a grandnephew of Josiah Bartlett of Kingston, signer of the Declaration of Independence. By 1804 he was associated with Hubbard C. Gale, a Concord cabinetmaker—possibly as an apprentice. In that year the youthful Bartlett was mentioned in Gale's advertisement as authorized to transact all business in the cabinetmaker's absence and "fulfil every engagement in the line of his business." The following year, shortly after Gale's untimely death, Bartlett advertised that he had taken over Gale's shop. In 1806 Bartlett opened a shop in Salisbury. He is described as a cabinetmaker in a deed of 1808. In that year the location of the Concord shop was changed from adjacent to opposite Gale's Tavern, as is indicated in existing labels. In 1809 Bartlett sold his business at both locations to cabinetmaker Porter Blanchard (q.v.); the furniture stock was not completely liquidated until 1811. Levi Bartlett had become a resident of Boston by 1814 when he married Clarissa Walker of Concord, daughter of Judge Timothy Walker. He advertised in an 1816 Concord newspaper as a Boston merchant, and is listed in an 1852 publication as one of the wealthiest men in Massachusetts.

BATCHELLER, Oliver (1791–1816)

Batcheller was one of a family of carpenter-cabinetmakers which included his father, Joseph, and three older brothers, Joseph, John Merry, and Hervey. Joseph and John were born in Marblehead, Massachusetts, in 1773 and 1775 respectively; the family moved to New Ipswich in 1780. Oliver Batcheller's cabinetmaking career was short-lived; he died unmarried and is buried in New Ipswich. His will, drawn less than three months before his death, left the bulk of his estate to his brother Hervey (including his "New Black Coat, Merseills Waistcoat, New Dimity striped Pantaloons") and to his two sisters. He also bequeathed twenty-five dollars to the New Ipswich Congregational Church "for the encouragement of Young Men preparing for preaching the Gospel as Missionaries."

## BLANCHARD, Ephraim (1778–1841)

Born in Billerica, Massachusetts, Blanchard evidently came to Lyndeboro with his family shortly after the Revolution; his father, Jotham, is listed in the 1790 and 1800 censuses of that town. Ephraim is identified as a cabinetmaker in Amherst land records as early as 1803. His first wife, Elizabeth Wilkins, had died at Provincetown, Massachusetts, in the preceding year, which may suggest that Blanchard was trained in Massachusetts.

Although most of Blanchard's known documented work is in the late Federal style, a labeled desk and bookcase in the exhibition (no. 37) bears the penciled date "24 July 18 1811." Beginning in the 1820s, he advertised a wide variety of cabinet wares. He was active in church and town affairs, serving on a committee to assign pews in the "New Meeting-house" in 1835 and as a selectman in 1836. The inventory of Blanchard's estate lists—in addition to extensive household furnishings—several pieces of unfinished furniture, a turning lathe and other shop tools, and paints, a paint stone, and paint dishes.

## BLANCHARD, Porter (1788–1871)

Born on 16 August 1788 in that part of Amherst which was later incorporated as Milford, he was not related to cabinetmaker Ephraim Blanchard (q.v.). In 1809, at the age of twenty-one, Porter Blanchard advertised that he had taken over the "cabinet manufactory" of Levi Bartlett (q.v.) in its two locations. The following year he married Anne (Nancy) Stickney Souther of Concord. He advertised in 1811 for two journeymen cabinetmakers to whom "instructions in the art of making Banding and Stringing" would be given. Blanchard was one of the original members of the Concord Mechanic's Association (1828) and worked as a cabinetmaker as late as 1834 with the assistance of his oldest son, Charles P. Blanchard. In 1839 C. P. Blanchard and Company's "Pulpit and Couch Manufactory" advertised as "successors to Porter Blanchard." Porter Blanchard devoted his later years to the large-scale manufacture of the renowned "Blanchard churn," and was also listed intermittently as a drum maker. After his death the manufacture of churns was continued by "Porter Blanchard's Sons," who are known to have shipped them around the world.

## BLISS & HORSWILL (1797–1798)

On 26 December 1797 Bliss and Horswill, "cabinet and chair makers, from Boston", advertised that they had "taken a stand in Charlestown." Until 23 March 1798 the partnership was composed of Thomas Bliss (q.v.) and John W. Horswill (q.v.). At that time two members were added and the name was changed to Bliss and Horswill, Watkins and Brown. The firm carried on the cabinet and chairmaking business in Woodstock, Vermont, as well as in Charlestown until 4 June 1798.

## BLISS, Thomas (1767–1839)

Born in Boston on 3 February 1767, Bliss was the son of a former shipwright; in June 1792 he married Priscilla Howe, who was born in Andover, Massachusetts. He undoubtedly received his training as a cabinetmaker in Boston. Between December 1797 and March 1798 he worked in the Connecticut Valley town of Charlestown with John W. Horswill (q.v.) in the cabinetmaking partnership of Bliss and Horswill (q.v.). From March to June 1798 he was a member of the firm of Bliss and Horswill, Watkins and Brown, which carried on the cabinetmaking business in Woodstock, Vermont, as well as in Charlestown. Afterward Bliss continued to work in Charlestown, advertising for a journeyman cabinetmaker in July 1799. About 1805 he moved to Auburn, New York. In 1836 he was shipwrecked on Lake Huron during a move to Allegan, Michigan, where he died.

## BOARDMAN, Langley (1774–1833)

Born in Ipswich, Massachusetts, and baptized there on 19 June 1774, he apparently served an apprenticeship in the Ipswich-Salem area. Boardman appeared in Ports-

# Langley Boardman

INFORMS his friends and the public, that he has ready-made and for sale at his shop in Ladd-street, a general assortment of Cabinet work, among which are the following:

Side-Boards; Secretaries and Book-Cases; Ladies Secretaries, Bureaus; Commodes; Card-Tables; Dining-Tables; Pembrook-Tables; Night Tables; Pot-Cubboards; Candle-Stands; Fire-Screens; Lolling Chairs; Eafy Chairs; and a variety of other articles which he will fell at the loweft prices for cafh.

As he is determined to leave this town on the 1ft of June next, any perfons who wifh to fupply themfelves in his line, are defired to call at his fhop previous to that date.

Portfmouth, April 5, 1799.

*New Hampshire Gazette* [Portsmouth], 16 April 1799.

mouth in 1798, working in a shop on Ladd Street. The following year he advertised a variety of furniture forms, including bureaus, night tables, and lolling chairs; and announced his impending departure from town on 1 June 1799. He married Rachel Annabel of Hamilton, Massachusetts (the daughter of a cabinetmaker), on 31 January 1801. Boardman established a shop on Ark Lane (Penhallow Street) in Portsmouth about 1801, and in 1803 moved to Congress Street where he later built the Franklin Block. He built an imposing wooden dwelling on Middle Street about 1804. He invested heavily in real estate and in a number of vessels; in banks, stage companies, the Piscataqua Bridge, and the Cocheco Manufacturing Company. Boardman served as president of the Associated Mechanics and Manufacturers of the State of New Hampshire and of the Piscataqua Bank, was a state senator and a member of the governor's council. His obituary states that he was "an industrious and successful mechanic —and was one of that small number, who, when wealth increases, do not abandon their

trades." The inventory of his shop lists some $1,600 worth of unfinished or unsold furniture.

## BRIGGS, Eliphalet (1788–1853)

Born in Keene on 22 February 1788, Briggs was part of a large family of cabinetmakers. His father, also named Eliphalet, and all five of his younger brothers are said to have been skilled at that trade. On 21 December 1810 Briggs married Lucy Brown of Packersfield (later Roxbury); in the same year, he opened a shop in Keene. During the next four decades, he was involved in a series of cabinetmaking partnerships, some including members of his family. Newspaper advertisements indicate that about 1819 Briggs began to supplement his cabinetmaking business with the sale of marble and gravestones; in 1843 he began to deal also in "Piano Fortes, from one of the best manufactories in this country." As late as 1849 the *New England Mercantile Union Business Directory* listed Eliphalet Briggs, in partnership with his son William S., as a furniture and chair manufacturer.

## CARLETON, Michael (1793–1876)

Born at Newbury, Vermont, he was the son of Dudley Carleton, a Massachusetts-born cabinetmaker who settled in Newbury during the Revolution. Michael is said to have moved across the Connecticut River to Haverhill in 1812. He married Betsy Putnam at Newbury in 1816. Carleton first purchased land in Haverhill in 1819; in April 1822 he advertised that he had "recently built a shop opposite J. Sinclair's tavern, where he intends to carry on the Cabinet Making Business in its various branches." He is listed in 1849 and 1856 New England business directories as furniture manufacturer and cabinetmaker respectively. Carleton and his oldest son, Michael, Jr., are identified in a Haverhill town history as cabinetmakers and wheelwrights.

## CARTER, Minot (1812–1873)

Born in Buckland, Massachusetts, he was the son of Benjamin Carter and Hepzibah Williams, who came from New Ipswich. Carter's sister Amanda married Josiah Prescott Wilder (q.v.) in 1826, and he is presumed to have moved to New Ipswich sometime after that date. Since he does not appear to have married or owned land there, he may have resided with another member of the family. Carter's name is entered in J. P. Wilder's daybook and ledger under date of 11 November 1837. There are several entries for 1841, and in September of that year Wilder noted a credit for "Chairs left in my possession when you left the business." Two styles of printed paper labels are known and both describe Carter as working "at Wilder's Chair Factory."

## CHOATE & MARTIN (1794–1796)

A cabinetmaking and chairmaking partnership which on 2 April 1794 announced the opening of a shop in Concord and, in January 1796, advertised for two journeymen cabinetmakers. The dissolution of the partnership of Robert Choate (q.v.) and George Whitefield Martin (q.v.) was declared on 16 May 1796.

## CHOATE, Robert (1770–?)

Born on 6 September 1770 in Newburyport, Massachusetts, Choate was in partnership in Concord with George Whitefield Martin (q.v.) of Marblehead, Massachusetts, from 1794 to 1796. He married Apphia Worthen in Concord on 1 September 1796. After the dissolution of the firm of Choate and Martin (q.v.), he continued alone in the cabinet and chairmaking business in Concord until about 1800. In that year he sold his property to George Whitefield Rogers (q.v.), another cabinetmaker originally from Newburyport. By 1807 the records of Grafton County included a Robert Choat of Orford, "cabinetmaker." He is said to have moved to Thetford, Vermont, where Apphia Choate died on 26 August 1809.

## DAMON, Benjamin (1783–1872)

Born on 22 December 1783 in Amherst, Damon was in partnership in Concord with

*New Hampshire Sentinel* [Keene], 13 February 1824.

William Low (q.v.) from 1806 to 1826. On 10 January 1811 he married Sophia Nichols of Amherst, the sister of William Low's wife. After the dissolution of the partnership of Low and Damon (q.v.), Damon continued alone in the chairmaking and painting business. As late as 1834 he advertised chairs "of my own manufacturing." He was one of the original members of the Concord Mechanic's Association (1828). By 1844 Damon was advertising as a house and sign painter, and continued working as a painter until a few years before his death.

## DINSMORE, James (working 1803–1823)

The birthplace of this Hopkinton cabinetmaker is unknown, but he may have received his training in the Goffstown-Bedford area. His inlay style is related to that of John Dunlap II (q.v.) of Antrim who is said to have been apprenticed to "a Mr. McAfee in Bedford." James Dinsmore later sold land to a William Dinsmore from Goffstown, which may indicate that he had family connections in that area. By 1803 Dinsmore was listed among the taxpayers of

Hopkinton; he advertised as a cabinetmaker in that place in 1805. On 9 December 1804 he married Mrs. Sally Eaton, widow of Hopkinton joiner Thomas Eaton. Sally Eaton Dinsmore is believed to have been the daughter of David Young (q.v.), a prolific Hopkinton joiner. It is possible that Dinsmore, as well as Ebenezer Virgin (q.v.) and Asa Kimball (q.v.) of Concord, was associated for a time with Young; Dinsmore and Young were listed consecutively in the 1803 highway tax list. By 1809, Dinsmore had removed to Brunswick, Maine, and was listed in deeds as a cabinetmaker there as late as 1823.

DUNLAP, John, II (1784–1869)

The son of Major John Dunlap of Bedford, John II was about eight years old at the time of his father's death and could not have learned cabinetmaking from him. According to family tradition, he was apprenticed about 1800 to "a Mr. McAfee in Bedford," probably David McAfee (1770–1809), who had worked seventy-eight days for Major John in 1786 "at the outside of William Riddles House." John II first purchased property in Antrim in 1806 and is identified as a cabinetmaker in land records. The town history states that he built a house and shop in that year and was in business for a long time. He is also said to have owned looms for weaving underclothing, a business he had learned in New York State in 1815. In June 1807 John II married Jennie (Jane) Nesmith of Antrim. Their two oldest sons died in a "spotted fever" epidemic in 1812, but the third, Robert (1813–1861), worked as a chair and cabinetmaker with his father after about 1835. Following the death of his first wife, John II married Abigail Spaulding of Hillsborough (1837). He is said to have moved to Ohio in 1844, but purchased land in Goffstown between 1851 and 1868 and eventually returned.

ELLIS, Horace (1807–?)

Born in Sutton on 5 March 1807, Ellis was the son of a physician who had moved with his family to Newport by 1810. In Edmund Wheeler's 1879 History of Newport he is listed among fourteen workmen employed by Willard Harris, one of the town's two largest furniture producers. Ellis may have been apprenticed to Harris, for the latter had advertised in 1825 for "a lad of 16 or 18 years of age." In November 1831, Harris sold his "Cabinet and Chair Shop, together with the whole of his stock," to Gilmore, Hall & Dwinel. The only known piece of furniture signed by Ellis is dated 1832. It is possible that he had recently completed a term as a journeyman in Massachusetts, for on 11 April 1832 one Horace Ellis—described as a resident of New Salem, Massachusetts—married Abigail Ober in Washington, near Newport. This couple is known to have settled in Auburn, Ohio; there are no references to Ellis in Newport area records after 1832.

FOLSOM, Abraham (1805–1886)

Born in Exeter on 19 September 1805, Abraham was distantly related to Josiah Folsom (q.v.), a Portsmouth chairmaker, and was

## Cabinets & Chairs.

### Choate & Martin,

Cabinet and Chair Makers,

BEG leave to inform their friends and the public, that they have opened a Shop oppofite Mr. *Harris's* Store in Concord, where they intend carrying on the bufinefs of making

## Cabinets, Chairs, &c.

in the various branches thereof, at a moderate price; and all thofe who pleafe to favour them with their commands, may depend on having their work done in the neateft and moft fafhionable manner, with punctuality and difpatch—and the fmalleft favours will be gratefully acknowledged.

Concord, April 2.       8

*A quantity of Cherry Boards wanted by faid Choate & Martin.*

*Courier of New Hampshire* [Concord], 10 April 1794.

*Political Observatory* [Walpole], 6 December 1805.

probably the A. Folsom who advertised in 1829 in Dover as a portrait and ornamental painter. Folsom married Abigail Smith Pierce of Dover on 5 September 1832. He advertised in 1836 a "Furniture, Chair and Paint Store" in Dover, together with "Sign and Ornamental Painting." Folsom advertised the sale of furniture until 1846, and afterward dealt in paints and oil only. He is believed to have been the same "Abram Folsom" who, in 1834, leased a mill in Rochester for the manufacture of chairs and was succeeded by Stephen Shorey (q.v.) in 1845. Folsom entered into successive partnerships with various members of his family; "A. Folsom & Co.", the only one of these firms whose name has been found stamped on chairs, flourished between 1845 and 1847. Before 1856 Folsom began the manufacture of oilcloth carpeting in Dover. By 1867 the headquarters of his oilcloth business had moved to Boston.

## FOLSOM, Josiah (1763–1837)

Born on 7 February 1763 in Dover, he was the son of a wigmaker. Folsom may have served his chairmaking apprenticeship in Boston, where he married Mary (Polly)

Perkins of Ipswich, Massachusetts, in 1786. He moved to Portsmouth in 1788 and in 1797 advertised Windsor chairs "of the best kind . . . as cheap as can be purchased in BOSTON", illustrating his notice with a woodcut of a bowback Windsor with an upholstered seat. Folsom's first wife died in 1800 and he married Sarah Hull of Durham in 1803. In the same year he joined other craftsmen of the Portsmouth area in founding the Associated Mechanics and Manufacturers of the State of New Hampshire. An advertisement of 1805 mentions "Mr. Folsom's Chair manufactory" on Broad (State) Street. Records consistently describe Folsom as a chairmaker, but he is said also to have manufactured cut nails. In 1812 he purchased land with a wharf and water privileges in Portsmouth, and dealt (as did his son-in-law, Josiah Gilman Folsom) in West India goods.

## GOODEN, Jeremiah (1793–1840)

Born in Londonderry, the son of David and Huldah (Morse) Gooden, Jeremiah came to Milford as a child. Identified as a joiner in land records as early as 1817, he is described as a cabinetmaker in the *History of Milford* (1901). Gooden lived and died in the "house next north of the railroad station" at East Milford. He married Betsy Perkins (1797–1854) of Brookline in 1818. Their three daughters married and settled in Milford; two of them were bequeathed furniture— "my bookcase and case of drawers under the same" and "my writing desk"—in Gooden's will dated 4 March 1840. The document identifies the testator as a joiner.

## GOULD, John, Jr. (1793–1840)

The son of a carpenter and Revolutionary soldier of New Ipswich, John, Jr., engaged in the business of cabinetmaking in that town. In the Hillsborough County land records he is first listed as a cabinetmaker in 1819. In 1823 he married Eliza Ann Appleton of Dublin; they had two children. Jonas Chickering, who later made pianos in Boston, was apprenticed to Gould; furniture attributed to Chickering, and bearing marked similarities to documented pieces by Gould, is owned in New Ipswich. In September 1832 Gould, "about to close his business of Cabinet Making," advertised an auction of his tools and stock. He and his wife died within ten days of each other in Boston, where they had gone for reasons of health. The inventory of Gould's estate lists extensive personal property and an assortment of tools including "Turning Chisels & Gouges . . . Patterns & Lumber in back Shop . . . Turning Lathe & appendages." Also listed are a watch lathe and watchmaker's tools and equipment as well as a watch sign, which suggest that he followed that trade at the time of his death.

## HAZEN, Moses, Jr. (1776–1837)

Born at Rowley, Massachusetts, the son of Moses Hazen (or Hazzen) and Rebecca Cheney, Moses, Jr., moved to Weare with his parents after the Revolution. He married Sarah Eastman (1771–1838) at Newton; two of their children were born at Bradford in 1803 and 1805, indicating the family's residence there during those years. Hazen is identified as a "joyner" of Weare in an 1805 deed of land to John Dow of Weare, also a joiner. He died at South Weare, and the inventory of his estate made in December 1837 includes "carpenters saws," augers, planes, bitstock, bits, chisels, and gouges. His assets were chiefly real property, but farm animals such as oxen, sheep, horses, and turkeys are also listed.

## HILL, Daniel A. (1811–1878)

Born in Winchester on 14 June 1811. Hill married Leonora B. Morrill who was born in 1816, probably in Deering. On 17 November 1842 he advertised in Concord a "Furniture and Looking Glass Ware-House . . . at the old stand of E[liot] A[shley] Hill," his older brother, who had operated a cabinetmaking business there since 1821. After the death of his first wife on 31 March 1847, Daniel Hill married Amanda A. Flanders in Corcord in November of the same year. He advertised as a "Manufacturer of Cabinet Furniture, Pulpits, Couches, and Looking Glasses," and offered "Coffins,

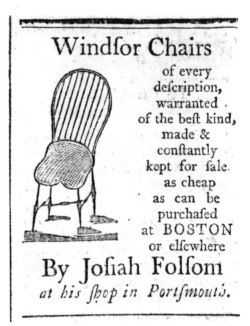

ready-made, or made to order at short notice." By 1860 five members of the Hill family were working for Daniel in Concord. Although in later years he was listed as a furniture dealer rather than manufacturer, in the record of his death his occupation is given as cabinetmaker.

## HOLMES, Andrew Paine (1816–1874)

The four sons of Joseph Holmes, a farmer and mason of Greenland, all became cabinetmakers. One of them, A. P. Holmes, went into business in 1848 with his brother Francis in Charlestown, Massachusetts, where the latter had learned the cabinetmaking trade. A. P. Holmes is listed in the *Manchester Directory* for 1852 as a furniture dealer. However, two years later he rejoined the firm of F. M. Holmes and Company in Charlestown, with which he was associated until 1872.

## HORSWILL, John W. (working 1797–1798)

Horswill was probably born in Rhode Island, the only state for which early census records list heads of families with this surname. Little is known of his life until he moved from Boston to New Hampshire, becoming a partner with Thomas Bliss (q.v.) in the cabinet and chairmaking firm of Bliss and Horswill (q.v.) in Charlestown from December 1797 to March 1798. Between March and June 1798 the larger firm of Bliss and Horswill, Watkins and Brown operated cabinetmaking shops in Charlestown and in Woodstock, Vermont. The subsequent career of Horswill is not known.

## HOUSTON, William (1755–1830)

The son of a Bedford blacksmith, Houston in March 1775 was apprenticed for two years to Major John Dunlap in order to learn "the Art or Mistry of a cabinett-maker and Joyner." The indenture specified that at the end of the apprenticeship Dunlap would "help him to make the Wooden part of a set of tools fit for the trade. . . ." However, Houston left in July 1776 to join the Revolutionary army, fighting under Stark at Bennington. He returned and worked for John Dunlap on the Zachariah Chandler house in Bedford in May and June 1777, paying taxes in that town in 1778. The following year Houston bought land in Peterborough, and is referred to as a joiner in the land records. He married (1) Elizabeth Miller in Litchfield in 1781; and (2) Isabel Campbell of Windham in Londonderry in 1799. About 1790 Houston moved to Antrim; he is called a "house-right" of Antrim in 1802 records.

## HUNT, Joseph Ruggles (1781–1871)

Born in Boston, Massachusetts, he was the son of Captain Abraham Hunt (a wine dealer) and his wife, Mary St. Leger. Joseph married Eleanor Tongue in 1803, and is said to have worked in Boston between 1805 and 1807. A family genealogy states that he resided in Cambridge in 1807 and transferred land there; he was identified as a cabinetmaker. Hunt probably settled in the portion of Eaton which is now Madison sometime after 1810; his name first appears in local records in an 1813 tax inventory. Two years later, identified as a chairmaker, he purchased land in Eaton, and in 1818 Joseph R.

Hunt, "cabinetmaker," acquired a mill site there. His son Elisha (b. 1807) may have joined him in the business; a land transfer of 1834 involving land and a shop identifies Elisha as a cabinetmaker. Hunt served in the state house of representatives in 1831 and 1832, and as postmaster of Eaton from 1841 to 1852; his name appears in local censuses until 1860.

## JUDKINS & SENTER (1808–1826)

This Portsmouth cabinetmaking firm was established in 1808 by Jonathan Judkins (q.v.) and William Senter (q.v.), and continued as a partnership until 9 September 1826, a few months before Senter's death. The firm operated at various locations on Broad (State) Street at different times. In 1812 John T. Senter, who was probably William's brother and who had first appeared in Portsmouth records in 1802, opened a turner's shop adjacent to the cabinet shop. The Judkins and Senter shop burned in the great Portsmouth fire of 22 December 1813, but within a month the firm was re-established in a new building on the same site, offering "Cabinet Furniture and Chairs of the newest fashion." In 1815, following John T. Senter's departure to join the army, Portsmouth chairmaker Henry Beck took "an apartment" in the Judkins and Senter shop, where he made, painted, and repaired chairs. During the 1820s the firm several times invited "Farmers' Daughters, and Fishermen's Wives" to exchange cider, potatoes, or fish for bureaus. At the dissolution of the partnership in 1826 the shop and stock-in-trade were appraised at $1,050. Thereafter, Judkins continued the business with his sons, while Beck remained in the same building until his retirement in 1828.

NOTICE
**To Farmers' Daughters, and** *Fishermen's Wives.*
JUDKINS & SENTER would like to exchange a few BUREAUS for FISH, POTATOES and CIDER.          Oct. 16.

*Portsmouth Journal*, 16 October 1824.

## JUDKINS, Jonathan (1780–1844)

Born in Salisbury, he was the son of Leonard Judkins, a prominent citizen of that town. Records differ regarding the year of Judkins' birth; the date used here is based on his death notice, which appeared in the *New Hampshire Gazette*. Judkins was probably trained as a cabinetmaker in Salisbury, where his father's farm adjoined that of Moses Bohonon, a cabinetmaker born a few years before Judkins. Judkins first appeared in Portsmouth in 1806, having been preceded there by his brother Leonard. In 1808 he formed a partnership with joiner William Senter (q.v.), opening a shop on Broad (State) Street. He married Lucy Maria Vaughan in Portsmouth in the same year, and built a house on Jaffrey (Court) Street in 1815. The dissolution of the partnership of Judkins and Senter (q.v.) was announced on 9 September 1826. Judkins continued the cabinetmaking business after Senter's death, being joined by his sons John, Leonard, Daniel V., and Samuel L. at various periods. The firm continued to make furniture, evidently with declining prosperity, until Judkins' death on 3 November 1844.

## KIMBALL, Asa (working about 1800)

There were two Asa Kimballs in Concord in the late eighteenth and early nineteenth centuries—Major Asa (1741–1804) and his son, Asa, Jr. (1767–1815). Both were born and died there, and were cousins of John Kimball, Concord cabinetmaker. It is not known which man produced the two known tall clock cases bearing the printed label "MADE BY Asa Kimball, CABINET & CHAIR MAKER, Concord, New Hampshire." Neither father nor son is identified in land or probate records as a joiner or cabinetmaker. However, one of Kimball's labeled clock cases is almost identical to examples made by David Young of Hopkinton (q.v.), and the other is similar to another type of Young case. In 1773 David Young married the sister of Major Asa Kimball's wife; it seems likely that the Concord cabinetmaker was Asa Kimball, Jr., who may have been associated for a time with his uncle. Asa, Jr.'s younger brother John is known to have removed to Hopkinton early in life and to

have become a joiner there. The only suggestion that Major Asa Kimball may have been the cabinetmaker is the use of a printed militia form as a dust shield inside the hood of one clock (see no. 18).

An Asa Kimball, possibly the same, advertised in 1798 as carrying on the cabinetmaking business in Dunbarton; a 1799 deed refers to this craftsman as a "shop joyner."

## KIMBALL, John (1739–1817)

Born in Bradford, Massachusetts, he was the son of Benjamin and Priscilla Hazen Kimball. A high chest of drawers in this exhibition (no. 14) establishes Kimball's presence in the Manchester area in 1762. In December 1764 he worked at laying a floor for the Reverend Timothy Walker of Rumford (now Concord), and the following February the name of John Kimball, "joiner", appeared on a deed as a new resident of Rumford. Kimball married Anna Ayer of Haverhill, Massachusetts, on 23 November 1765; they had eight children, all born in Concord. He served on the Committee of Safety in 1777 and 1778, and was a deacon in the First Congregational Church from 1789 until his death. Styling himself a "joiner," Kimball was one of three carpenters and joiners who gave land to the town in 1802 for an addition to the meetinghouse.

An account book preserved in the family and covering the years from 1790 to 1816 suggests the range of Kimball's activities during this period. Entries for such routine joiner's tasks as making and mending window sash are interspersed with references to making and repairing articles of furniture. Kimball had accounts with clockmakers Timothy Chandler and Levi and Abel Hutchins and with Cabinetmaker George W. Rogers (q.v.).

## LOW & DAMON (c. 1806–1826)

Both members of this chairmaking and painting partnership came to Concord from Amherst about 1806. Before settling in Concord, William Low (q.v.) and Benjamin Damon (q.v.) may have been associated with Daniel Abbot of Peterborough, one of the few chairmakers known to have been working

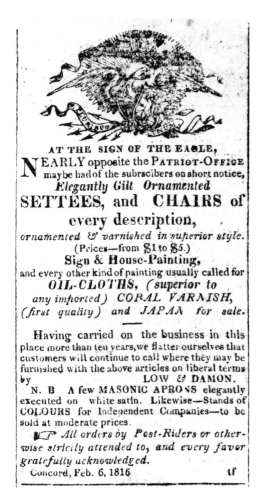

*New-Hampshire Patriot* [Concord], 6 February 1816.

in the Amherst area about 1800. Soon after their arrival in Concord, Low and Damon are said to have acquired about one hundred unpainted chairs from Peterborough. During the years of the partnership, Low apparently specialized in painting, Damon in chairmaking. One of their most important commissions was for the State House (constructed between 1816 and 1819); in addition to providing chairs for the interior, Low and Damon served as the major painting contractor for the building. The partnership was dissolved on 14 January 1826.

LOW, William (1779–1847)

Born on 20 April 1779 in Amherst, Low married Grace Gardner Nichols of Amherst

on 8 June 1803. He was in partnership in Concord with Benjamin Damon (q.v.) from 1806 to 1826. Low is described in an 1806 deed as "Painter & Chairmaker," but thereafter is identified as painter only. He was one of the three-member building committee (1816–1820) for the State House. After the dissolution of the firm of Low and Damon (q.v.), Low opened a furniture warehouse in Concord where he sold chairs "of Boston and New-York manufacture." He served as Concord's postmaster from 1829 to 1839. Low is listed in the 1830 city directory as both painter and postmaster, but apparently gave up his trade shortly afterward to concentrate on public affairs.

MALLARD, Ephraim (1789–1874)

Born in Tuftonboro on 20 April 1789, he began to work at the age of twenty-one for James Chase, a cabinetmaker in that part of Gilmanton incorporated as Gilford in 1812. It seems likely that Mallard had formerly been apprenticed to Chase. According to the latter's account books, Mallard rented a shop from Chase in 1811 and 1812 and paid his board partly by making furniture for him. Ephraim's older brother Henery also worked for Chase. On 30 July 1816 Ephraim married Clarisa Muservy (Merserve) in Gilford. After his first wife hanged herself in 1837, he married Mercy Barker of Strafford on 23 December 1838. Mallard is listed in an 1849 business directory as a furniture manufacturer of Meredith Bridge (a village then partly in Gilford and later known as Laconia) and in the 1850 census as a Gilford cabinetmaker.

MARTIN, George Whitefield (1771–1810)

Baptized in Marblehead, Massachusetts, on 5 May 1771, Martin is listed as a cabinetmaker in Priscilla Sawyer Lord and Virginia Clegg Gamage, *Marblehead: The Spirit of '76 Lives Here* (Philadelphia, 1972). He was in partnership in Concord with Robert Choate (q.v.) from Newburyport, Massachusetts, between 1794 and 1796. After the dissolution of the partnership of Choate and Martin (q.v.), Martin apparently returned to Essex County, Massachusetts, settling in Salem where he married Sally Bullock in April 1797. After his death his cabinetmaking shop and tools were sold at auction.

## OSBORN, Moses, Jr. (1796–1870)

Seventh of the eleven children of Moses and Ruth (Paige) Osborn—Quakers who were resident in Weare by September 1785—Moses, Jr., was nineteen when his father died. In 1821 he is identified in land records as a "cordwainer," but beginning in 1827 when he purchased property "also containing a paint shop" from chairmaker Leonard Gee, he is termed a "joiner." In land transactions of July 1831 he is called both cabinetmaker and joiner. The town history states that he built a cabinet shop near Weare Center, and "made excellent furniture, about 1825," and that he operated a tannery. Moses, Jr., married (1) Phebe Stuart on 28 September 1837; and (2) Eliza Hussey on 24 October 1844. Genealogical references indicate that he lived in Winslow, Maine; he probably removed there about 1845, the date of his last land transfers in Weare.

## PARKER, Robert (1797–1844)

Born on 13 May 1797 in Bedford, he was the son of William and Nabby (Parker) Parker. He married (1) Charlotte Chamberlain; and (2) Mille Rand. Parker first paid taxes in Bedford in 1819, and at about that time his future brother-in-law, John Rand (1800–1873), who later became an internationally-known portrait painter, was apprenticed to him to learn the trade of cabinetmaking. On 14 July 1823 Parker announced his partnership in cabinetmaking with Jesse Richardson, at the shop formerly occupied by Rand and Richardson in Piscataquog Village, in the northeastern section of Bedford. In 1835 he advertised for a journeyman and an apprentice. The inventory of Parker's estate, authorized on 1 October 1844, includes planes, chisels, gouges, compasses, "Lot Wood Knobs," hardware, turning tools, "Lot furniture partly manufactured," bed-screws, and "1 Paint mill & Stone . . . all other painting tools & paints." The last-named items were among those selected as

the widow's portion, but the other tools were apparently sold at auction with the balance of Parker's household goods.

## ROGERS, George Whitefield (1770–1847)

Born in Newburyport, Massachusetts, on 23 October 1770, he married Lucy Farnham there on 14 February 1796. In 1800 Rogers bought property in Concord from Robert Choate (q.v.), a Concord cabinetmaker also born in Newburyport. Announcing the following year that he had taken "the shop lately occupied by Mr. Robert Choate," he continued to advertise as a cabinetmaker until 1815. In 1819 the shop was offered for sale, and his house was sold at auction in 1821. The next year Rogers and his wife were admitted to church membership in Alfred, Maine, by a letter of dismissal from Concord. He is called "cabinetmaker" in deeds of York County, Maine. Among his documented pieces is a chest of drawers bearing a printed Alfred label dated 1821.

## ROSS, Stephen (1785–?)

Born in Gilmanton on 16 September 1785, Stephen was the son of Jonathan Ross, a Gilmanton cabinetmaker who first appeared in Strafford County land records in 1776 as a "cabinetmaker" of Salem, Massachusetts. Stephen's half-brother, Jonathan, Jr. (b. 1772), and his cousin, Samuel Dudley (b. 1773), were also Gilmanton cabinetmakers. By 1809 Stephen had settled in Salisbury, where he married Sarah Peterson on 22 October. On 26 January 1813 he advertised the products of his Salisbury cabinet shop in the *Concord Gazette*. He is referred to in deeds from 1810 to 1818 as a cabinetmaker of Salisbury, but as early as 1815 his farm and shop were advertised for sale. The following year he sold land in Salisbury to William Parsons of Pittsfield, a cabinetmaker who had been born in Gilmanton and was closely related to Ross through marriage. The Salisbury Baptist Church records state that Stephen and Sarah Ross were "dismissed to Ogden . . . N.Y." Both are listed in historical accounts of this Erie Canal town as among the first members of the Baptist church organized there in 1819.

## SENTER, William (1783–1827)

Probably born in Londonderry or Windham, he may have been apprenticed in Portsmouth, where he appeared on the tax lists as a joiner in 1804 at the age of twenty-one. In 1808 Senter and Jonathan Judkins (q.v.) formed a cabinetmaking partnership, opening a shop on Broad (State) Street. In the same year Senter married Dolly Gerrish in Portsmouth. He built a house on Cabot Street in 1814, and was active in town affairs. The dissolution of the partnership of Judkins and Senter (q.v.) was announced on 9 September 1826, probably because of the latter's ill health. At his death in January 1827 Senter retained a half interest in the cabinet shop, appraised at $525.

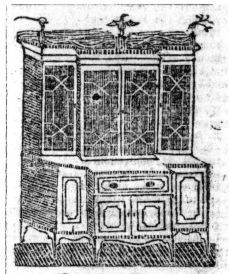

**Stephen Ross,**

INFORMS his friends and the public, that he has on hand and keeps constantly made by him, at his SHOP, about one mile West of the Academy, in Salisbury, a good assortment of
**CABINET FURNITURE
AND CHAIRS,**
in the newest fashion, which he will warrant as good, and will sell as cheap for Cash or produce, as any in the country. And a handsome discount in the price, will be made for ready pay.
ALSO,
Furniture repaired and Varnished at a reasonable price.
Salisbury, N. H. Jan. 26, 1813. 36

*Concord Gazette,* 9 February 1813.

## SHOREY, Stephen (1808?–1879)

Born in Lebanon, Maine, Shorey is said to have been one of the first settlers of East Rochester, and to have operated a saw and grist mill there beginning about 1825. He married Louisa Corson, whose family was also involved in the mills. From 1845 to 1862 "Shorey's Mills" included a chair manufactory, apparently that formerly operated by Abraham Folsom (q.v.) of Dover. Under Shorey's ownership the mill produced three to four thousand chairs a year. Shorey also owned the only store in East Rochester. Directories later (1868–1878) list him as a lumber dealer.

## STANTON, Elijah (c. 1820–?)

Stanton's name first appears in Carroll County land records in 1842; his occupation is given as cabinetmaker. In the *New England Mercantile Union Business Directory* for 1849 the list of furniture manufacturers includes "E. Stanton & Co." of Conway. According to information in the 1850 census, Stanton, a cabinetmaker, was born in New Hampshire about 1820. In 1852 he, John McMillan, and Timothy Wolcott, "trader", were "joint partners negotiating business under the firm name of John McMillan & Co." The nature of the business is not specified, but the partnership is recorded as having purchased land near Stanton's cabinet shop. An 1858 land transfer describes Stanton as "Gentleman," and the census of 1860 lists him as a farmer. These changes suggest that he may have become inactive as a cabinetmaker by 1860.

## VIRGIN, Ebenezer (1767–1842?)

Born in Concord on 15 March 1767, the son of William Virgin, he was frequently referred to as Ebenezer Virgin, "Jr.," in order to distinguish him from his uncle, "Lieut." Ebenezer Virgin. At the age of twenty-one, he married Elizabeth Quinby of Hopkinton, and he was listed as residing there. It seems likely that he had just completed an apprenticeship in that town, where David Young (q.v.) was active as a joiner. Virgin had moved to Concord by the time his second child was born in 1789. He was taxed in Concord from 1792 to 1798 and appointed surveyor of lumber in 1794. A 1795 deed identifies him as "Ebenezer Virgin Jun. of Concord, Joiner." Virgin advertised in a Concord newspaper on 1 January 1796 for "an Apprentice to The Joiner's Business." He had moved to Rumford, Maine, by 1799 and married Polly Gibson of Brownfield, Maine, in 1813. An "Eben Virgin" is recorded as having died in Rumford in 1842.

At least two of Ebenezer's brothers, William and Simeon, were also joiners. Their grandfather, also named Ebenezer Virgin (d. 1766) and one of the earliest settlers in Concord, is said to have been a cabinetmaker.

## WETHERBEE, Abijah (1781–1835)

Probably born in Lunenburg, Massachusetts, Abijah Wetherbee married Elizabeth Wilder (1784–1861), sister of Joseph (q.v.) and Josiah Prescott Wilder (q.v.). The date of the marriage is not known, but the birth of a daughter is recorded in Boston in 1807, the year in which Peter and Joseph Wilder "of Boston" purchased land in New Ipswich. Wetherbee probably arrived in New Ipswich with, or shortly after, his father-in-law and brother-in-law, although his name is not listed in land records before 1813 when he is identified as a chairmaker resident in that place. Kidder and Gould's *History of New Ipswich* (1852) refers to Wetherbee as a "partner" with Peter Wilder and his sons Josiah Prescott and John B. Wilder in the chairmaking business.

## WILDER, Isaiah (1782–1867)

Born on 23 March 1782 in Hingham, Massachusetts, Wilder was the son of Isaiah and Susan (Leavitt) Wilder and a cousin of the well-known Hingham clockmaker Joshua Wilder. On 19 March 1809 Isaiah, Jr. (as he was known in his youth), married Salome Ramsdel in nearby Pembroke, Massachusetts. He is said to have "followed the sea in early life," but was described as a "cabinetmaker of Hingham" in 1821 when he purchased land in Surry. There are several references to Isaiah Wilder in Surry town records between 1823 and 1826. By 1828 he

had moved to Keene, but was not directly related to the Wilder family of furniture makers active in Keene and New Ipswich. In December 1849 Wilder was married in Attleboro, Massachusetts, to Lydia Daggett, his first wife having died in Keene the previous January. The marriage record refers to him as a "farmer" of New Hampshire, suggesting that he had given up his cabinetmaking trade. Wilder may have moved out of state temporarily, for when he died on 11 October 1867 in Gilsum he was described as "formerly of Attleboro, Mass."

## WILDER, Joseph (1787–1825)

Born in Keene, he was the oldest son of Peter Wilder (1761–1841), patriarch of the chairmaking dynasty in and around New Ipswich. Peter's older brother Abijah was a cabinetmaker in Keene, having emigrated to that town from Lancaster, Massachusetts, but whether the two worked together is not known. A family genealogy states that Peter worked as a chairmaker at Lancaster and Boston before moving to New Ipswich. Joseph and Peter, identified as tradesmen of Boston, purchased land in New Ipswich in

**DANIEL A. HILL,**
MANUFACTURER OF
## CABINET FURNITURE,
## PULPITS, COUCHES,
AND LOOKING-GLASSES;
Palm Leaf and Hair Mattresses;
Chairs of all kinds, cheap;
VANEARS, and LOOKING-GLASS PLATES,
At the Shop lately occupied by **Eliot A. Hill,**
198 Main Street, nearly opposite the American House.

David Watson, *A Directory . . . of . . . Concord Centre Village,* 1844.

1807. The family settled in the northwestern corner of the town, in the vicinity of "Tophet Swamp"; the settlement later became known as "Wilder's Village" and is so styled in contemporary records and maps. Other chairmaking members of the family include Thomas (1791–1862), Josiah Prescott (q.v.), John B. (1804–1852), and Calvin R. (1806–1852). Joseph Wilder's brothers-in-law Abijah Wetherbee (q.v.) and Minot Carter (q.v.) were also engaged in the chairmaking business.

## WILDER, Josiah Prescott (1801–1873)

This was the most prolific of the chairmaker sons of Peter Wilder, to judge from the comparatively large number of examples stamped "J. P. WILDER. / WARRANTED" that have been located. Born at Boston, Josiah Prescott (or J.P. as he came to be known) came to New Ipswich as a boy. He married Amanda Carter (1797–1851), sister of Minot Carter (q.v.), in 1826. After her death, he married Mary Ann Lovejoy of Wilton. A son, Josiah, Jr. (1832–1863), who settled in the Midwest, continued the chairmaking tradition to the next generation.

The volume and scope of J. P. Wilder's business is suggested by entries in his daybook and ledger (1837–1858), and in a journal (1839–1851) that documents his partnership with George P. Gardner (1839–1841). References to "Chairs sold on pedling excusion" (1838) and numerous entries recording sales of chairs in quantity to his brother Calvin's firm, Wilder and Stewart of New York City, or to retailers in Lowell, Massachusetts, indicate a wide market.

Wilder also had extensive dealings with his younger brother, John B. (1804–1852), who was paid for chair parts in quantity and for painting chairs. In his plans for 1847 J. P. Wilder noted, "It is my intention to do no more custom work or as little as possible, but confine myself to my customers in Lowell with the expectation that they will want what chairs I shall be able to manufacture." Frequent entries for "common chairs" are interspersed with references to "settee cradles," double back chairs, table chairs, "grecian stools," barroom chairs, and office chairs.

## YOUNG, David (1746?–1836?)

Probably born on 13 July 1746 in Kingston, he married Sarah Eastman in 1773 in Concord, where their first two children were born. Young signed the Association Test in Hopkinton in 1776. Ten years later he joined the Hopkinton Baptist Church, the manuscript records of which list his death date as 10 December 1836. Young is described in numerous land transactions as "joiner" and, beginning in 1801, occasionally as "cabinetmaker." Between 1816 and 1822 Edmund Currier, a Hopkinton clockmaker and silversmith whose account book survives, purchased from Young numerous clock and timepiece cases, together with a bedstead. In exchange, Young bought "clock trimmings," glasses, locks, and escutcheons from Currier. Young's son David (b. 1784) was also a cabinetmaker; and Ammi Burnham Young, the mid-nineteenth-century architect, is believed to have been his grandson.